Writing and Presenting in English:
The Rosetta Stone of Science

Writing and Presenting in English: The Rosetta Stone of Science

PETEY YOUNG

Professor Emerita
Southern Oregon University
Ashland, OR, U.S.A.

ELSEVIER

AMSTERDAM • BOSTON • HEIDELBERG • LONDON
NEW YORK • OXFORD • PARIS • SAN DIEGO
SAN FRANCISCO • SINGAPORE • SYDNEY • TOKYO

Elsevier
Radarweg 29, PO Box 211, 1000 AE Amsterdam, The Netherlands
The Boulevard, Langford Lane, Kidlington, Oxford OX5 1GB, UK

First edition 2006
Reprinted 2007

British Library Cataloguing in Publication Data
A catalogue record for this book is available from the British Library

Library of Congress Cataloging-in-Publication Data
A catalog record for this book is available from the Library of Congress

ISBN–13: 978-0-444-52118-7
ISBN–10: 0-444-52118-6

For information on all Elsevier publications
visit our website at books.elsevier.com

Working together to grow
libraries in developing countries
www.elsevier.com | www.bookaid.org | www.sabre.org

ELSEVIER   BOOK AID
            International   Sabre Foundation

Transferred to Digital Printing in 2008

Contents

Preface

This book is written specifically for scientists who have received formal education in speaking and writing English but for whom English is not a native nor an easily comfortable language. Those who have already published research in English, and those who have successfully presented at international conferences may well find the material in the book overly simplistic. The author apologizes to any such readers.

The quotations and proverbs throughout the book are at the whim of the author in the hope that English will continue to retain some of its beauty and mystery even though we now carefully discipline ourselves to present scientific results only in clear unambiguous language.

– Petey Young
August 2005
Vancouver BC, Canada

Peace to this meeting, wherefore we are met.
– Shakespeare
Henry V
Act VI, scene ii

– 1 –

Introduction

The Rosetta Stone, key to the original deciphering of Egyptian hieroglyphs, has probably been the most famous language inscription on the planet. This massive piece of polished black stone, discovered in 1799, contains parallel messages in old Greek, hieroglyphs, and demotic, a cursive form of hieroglyphics, chiseled into its surface. Twenty-four years after its discovery linguists finally completed the decoding which permitted the people of the world to understand the writings and culture of ancient Egypt.

> *O, wonder!*
> *. . . O brave new world.*
> *That has such people in it!*
>
>   *– Shakespeare*
>   *The Tempest*
>   *Act V, scene i*

Today the giant stone rests in the British Museum, waiting to inspire all scientists to translate their research results into a language that can be widely read. This is important for all of us because the science done in every country deserves reading by as many other scientists as possible.

Your personal Rosetta Stone for translating your science for others now has English as well as your native language inscribed on it. Native speakers blush in embarrassment but the world language today, the *lingua franca*, is English.

OPTIONS OTHER THAN ENGLISH

What? English? English, that complicated, irregular, jumbled, polyglot of a language? Surely there are finer languages:

- Why not German, the language once essential to any scientist who wanted to keep informed? German, a language which cannot be mumbled or slurred as native speakers daily do in English. German, which requires us to bend our mouths and tongues to the precision of its vowels and consonants and rewards us with the consistent spelling English lacks.
- And whatever happened to elegant French? Why not continue to give the world the fluid grace of French, with its consistency, sophistication, and mournful-sounding vowels?
- Why not Arabic, supremely expressive, with the world's most beautiful writing system?
- How about Russian with its passion and depth?
- Would it not be wonderful if science could have the orthographic efficiency of Japanese?
- Or if we all embraced the warmth of Spanish, with its smiling /ee/ sounds that almost hurt the cheeks with happiness.

- Or Hebrew, a language in which one can argue for hours and hours.
- Probably to be fair we should choose Esperanto so that everyone would be equally disadvantaged!

No, sorry, but despite all these and many other appealing options, the world, bar some unforeseeable catastrophic political development, is stuck with that most awkward of all languages, English. Perhaps this is evidence that the universe has a sense of humor.

It is linguistically illogical, but English has now become the Rosetta Stone of science, the language used to translate the science of the world into communication for the whole world.

Most of us learned classical English in school. Many of us learned it extremely well. However, trying to publish in science using the English we were taught in school is like trying to unlock one door with the key to another: the door never opens. English today is startlingly different from the English we learned in school, and, to make it worse, English is changing more rapidly today than ever before (Crystal, 2001).

To learn another language is to develop another soul . . .
– Czech proverb

A BIT OF HISTORY AND A WARNING

English has been adding words, adding new expressions, and changing meanings at an astonishing rate. This has been an exponential change post World War II – an expansion and change not seen since the language explosion of the 1100s–1300s. The English college dictionaries of the 1940s added words such as cybernetics, genocide, globalism, H-bomb, TV, radar, and accepted the use of a number of nouns as verbs; the 1950s added antimatter, bionics, ecosphere, microcircuit, nanosecond, and took in multiple words from other languages; the 1960s added biodegradable, jet lag, macrobiotics, megabyte, microchip, quark, and modified words to overcome cultural bias. In the 1970s the rate of new words in English increased even more rapidly as the language enlarged to include not only new technology but new social concepts.

By the 1990s communication through the Internet began what now appear to be irreversible changes in simplifying English through acceptance of more abbreviations, acronyms, and the non-alphabetic symbols now common in what David Crystal (2001) calls computer-mediated communication. English has always assimilated concepts and consequently words from other languages: 'tycoon', 'sheik', 'salsa', 'mocha', 'macho', 'pizza', 'steppe', 'rodeo', 'karate', 'sofa', 'mariachi', 'vodka', 'jihad', 'mullah', 'perestroika', 'Sandinista', 'burka', 'karaoke'. No end of this is foreseen by linguists.

ENGLISH TODAY

English today is a rapidly developing language, deeply influenced by Internet communication. As early as in the 1997 edition, the preface to the conservative *Random House Webster's College Dictionary* refers to the English language not as English, nor British English, or American English, but as 'world language'. By 2005 English had become the:

- language of international air traffic,
- favored language of diplomacy,
- lingua franca of the Internet and the World Wide Web, and
- language in which the world's best scientists need to publish.

> *At one time international English was limited to 'Hi', 'OK', 'Coca-Cola', 'Fanta', and 'taxi' . . .*

Change has been accelerated by the growth of the World Wide Web and the increasing pressure for rapid, clear communication via email. Use of tense has been becoming less complicated and less subtle in meaning. [See Chapter 4.] Today simple present tense and simple past tense are most common and the subtle, conditional, easily misinterpreted tenses involving words such as, 'should', 'could', 'would', 'might', 'may', 'can' are only seen infrequently.

Characteristics of English

One of the qualities that contributes to the ability of English to become a world language is that English is generous (many would say overly generous) in its acceptance and invention of new words and is quite nonchalant about changing syntax whenever traditional grammar gets in the way of cultural change. Writing about recent changes in the English language, one of the world's foremost authorities on language calls the current development a 'linguistic revolution' (Crystal, 2001). However, whether the current change is a revolution; whether it isn't; whether we like it; or whether we loathe it: English has changed and is continuing to change. It is no longer the English we learned in school or the English of yesterday's science journals.

Much of our training in English has encouraged us to learn to write in elegant, beautiful, often complicated ways. In school we gave our best efforts to produce words that would add glory to our meaning and delight to our teachers' hearts. Unfortunately this is not the way to the hearts of editors of today's science journals.

Please don't despair. Even if flowing exotic language is, unfortunately, not a good way to report research results, it is still a splendid way to write short stories, novels, and poetry. Perhaps English literature will forever have stirring pages filled with fiery words designed to inflame a reader's soul or poetry of soaring words intended to make one drunk with beauty. But these are not the words in which to report scientific results. Instead research is best served as if it were a meal, carefully prepared, arranged in an exact manner on a plate, and served cold.

Science Writing Today

Successful scientific writing today is done in a simple and direct fashion. First, the sequence must be precisely organized – not an easy thing to accomplish because so many things at first seem to need to be said simultaneously. Second, every sentence must be worded so that it is clear, with no alternate meanings available to innocent readers who were not in the lab with you, and therefore must rely only on the accuracy of your words.

Chapter 1

This book is designed to help non-English speaking scientists go beyond the knowledge in the weighty volumes of grammar from which they learned and:

- translate their scientific results into clear contemporary English,
- write articles suitable for publication,
- present their ideas at conferences, and, above all,
- maintain their joy of life.

> *These our actors,*
> *As I foretold you, were all spirits and*
> *Are melted into air, into thin air;*
> *And like the baseless fabric of this vision,*
> *The cloud-capped towers, the gorgeous palaces . . .*
> *— Shakespeare*
> *The Tempest*
> *Act IV, scene i*

PART I

Writing Research Articles for Publication

Every scientist in the world who is doing valuable research owes it to the world to publish clear, concise results. Only when these are published internationally will other scientists doing similar research be able to know what is being done elsewhere.

Part I contains information about the art of writing articles for publication to help you get published in an international journal.

- Chapter 2 gives you a model for self-analysis to help you construct a data bank that will give you the detailed help that fits your own individual writing needs.
- Chapter 3 guides you in ways to edit your writing successfully.
- Chapter 4 explains recent changes largely due to the influence of the Internet, and suggests new changes that are coming.
- Chapter 5 deals with writing abstracts, proposals, and cover letters.

The fact that we speak and write to each other in English does not mean we should conduct our mental explorations in English, for other languages may have patterns of thought vital for the future development of science. So let scientists communicate among countries in English but without losing the riches within their native languages.

– 2 –

The Art of Creating a Model to Help You Write

Models for writing science today cannot be found in grammar textbooks, most of which were published too long ago. Nor are they taught by English teachers who were educated some years ago by teachers educated before them and using texts written even earlier. None of these formerly good sources are helpful for writing scientific articles in today's rapidly changing, dynamic English. Actually, few, if any, of us received English instruction specifically designed for writing science.

Those of us who know how to write for science journals taught ourselves, slowly, and usually after several failures. In school we were taught how to use correct grammar and to write traditional, formal, English narratives. Our teachers taught us how to use allusions, metaphors, creative adjectives, and graceful expressions. We labored to produce lengthy, flowing language to delight our English teacher's heart. Unfortunately this is not the type of language that delights the hearts of science editors.

> *Think, when we talk of horses, that you see them?*
> *— Shakespeare*
> *Henry V*
> *Prologue*

Editors of science journals today want all ideas in language that is directly to-the-point, straightforward, and in as few words as possible. They want everything expressed with such clarity the science will be clear to all their readers. When your work is published, people all over the world will be reading your article. You not only want the meaning to be clear to them, but you want to represent your country well.

Today's science journals receive many articles reporting good scientific research but written in poor English. If the English is poor enough, the article is rejected; if the English is good enough, editors will decide whether or not the research is worth publishing. If the research seems worth publishing despite the poor English, the journal will sometimes have the article edited to make it acceptable, but this is becoming less common. The most common response of editors is to reject the paper.

> *Good prose is like a window pane.*
> *— George Orwell, 1903–50*

Science editors grieve over their lack of time and people to edit the English in their journals, because it is vital to them that their language standards are high. However, even with their continuous effort to publish only good English, the pressure to publish new research developments as rapidly as possible permits some poor language to appear in even the best science journals. This is tragic for two reasons: First, everyone wants the articles in widely-read journals to be understood clearly by readers all over the world, and second, no one wants new research to remain unpublished because editors simply did not understand the English in which it was written. Currently it is possible for good scientists in some countries or institutions to acquire an unwanted reputation for writing poor English. Don't let this happen to your country or institution. You are going to teach yourself to write so well that future editors will respond in joy when they see an article written by someone from your country.

Now, you ask, where can you find a model to help you write? Fortunately this is easy to answer.

FINDING DATA FOR YOUR MODEL

The very international journals in which you desire to be published contain the data for your model. Although the editors of such journals are seldom willing to edit any of the English sent to them, you can use their expertise if you are clever. The recent research articles in their journals have passed their standards and await your analysis. All you need to do is to find articles written by native English speakers and published in recent international journals. In these articles you will find gold mines of excellent information about contemporary scientific English: In them you can find excellent, up-to-date teachers who can be found nowhere else.

Each issue in every well-known, international, English-speaking journal contains several research articles written by authors at least one of whom is a native English speaker. Each of these presents excellent information to use in your own writing. They lie before you, waiting for you to turn on your analytical skills. The friendly, personal model for contemporary scientific writing that can be created using this information would be of help both to scientists who are not native speakers of English and unpublished scientists who are native speakers.

Your goal will be to get help from the language, not the science, in the articles. The first trick will be to insure that you have chosen excellent articles. The science of every article in a reputable, well-known international journal is sound, but the language may not be. So how will you know if you have found articles which will help you create a good model?

> *I see you stand like greyhounds in the slips,*
> *Straining upon the start.*
>
> *– Shakespeare*
> *Richard III*
> *Act I, scene i*

Characteristics of the Articles You Want to Find

In order to be worth the time you are going to put in analyzing them, articles you choose must have three basic characteristics:

- Each must be published in well-known international journals. Good examples of journals you might consider include: *Science, Nature, Biochemistry, Journal of the American Chemical Society, Angewandte Chemie, International*

Edition in English, Physical Review, Scientific American, and other highly-respected international journals specific to your field.

- Each must have been published within the last 3–5 years, no longer ago, sorry. Remember scientific language is in a rapid change process.
- Each must have at least one author who is a native speaker of English. This is particularly important. Usually the first author's name listed is the author most responsible for the writing, but not always. If one of the authors is a native speaker of English, probably that person has at least edited the writing. If none of the authors appear to be native speakers of English, the information about the data you draw from the structure of language in the article may easily be misleading.

All three of these characteristics are necessary so that the articles you choose will give you good data on the use and style of language. Surprisingly enough, you do not need to be concerned with the actual scientific content of the articles. Although the closer the article is to the science you do, the more specific language help it may yield about the language for specific procedures and results, this is not a vital characteristic of the articles you choose. You are searching for excellent material from which to create a good model.

CREATING YOUR MODEL

You are about to learn how to create your own system for analyzing the language used today in successful articles. Luckily, you are the type of person who can do this because you are a scientist, and scientists analyze well. First of all, by using a keen eye as you begin to study the language structure of current articles in international science journals, you will discover new things you may not have noticed before. You will realize:

- Science calls for a sudden narrative.
- Successful articles are dramatic stories told in as few words as possible.
- Above all, in the voice of science, clarity is crucial.

Your first step is to photocopy 1–3 articles all of which have the three characteristics mentioned earlier. Next you are going to design spreadsheets, either on paper or in your computer, on which to put the data you collect from the articles. Typically the kinds of information these spreadsheets contain include data on:

- Length and variety of sentence structure, including frequency of prepositional phrases.
- Use of transitions, direct and implied.
- Appropriate choice of verbs.
- Verb tenses.
- How articles begin and end.
- How and when to give credit to other researchers.

The actual topics you use for your spreadsheets, and the number of spreadsheets you make, will depend on the type of help you need and upon how sophisticated your English is. Someone else's spreadsheets would probably be of little or no value to you. However, here is an explanation of the type of data found on some typical spreadsheets:

Spreadsheet #1

This spreadsheet may contain notes on the lengths of sentences in the articles and on the variety of sentence structures. For example, check how frequently sentences start with the subject. Make notes about what words or structures sentences start with when they do not start with the subject. Write down particular structures that catch your eye as effective. Notice how infrequently prepositional phrases are used and when they are used. You may want to eliminate a number of irrelevant ones you find in your manuscript.

Spreadsheet #2

This spreadsheet may list and explain the transitions you find in your articles. Good use of transitions is vital to a well-written article, but good writers only use transitions appropriately. Make notes on when the transitions are used and notice how the meaning of the transition fits the meaning of the sentence. Check how frequently transitions are used and if the same one is used repeatedly or consecutively. [Table 3.1 displays some common transitions]

Spreadsheet #3

This spreadsheet may contain a list of appropriate varieties of the verbs you find along with notes about the situations in which they were used. Finding correct, varied, and interesting verbs to use in sentences about research procedures is one the most difficult writing problems a scientist encounters. The accuracy of the meaning of your sentences and paragraphs will be driven by the choice you make of verbs. This list will be valuable to you. Use it and keep adding to it.

> *Though this be madness, yet there is method in it*
> *– Shakespeare*
> *Hamlet*
> *Act II, scene i*

Spreadsheet #4

This spreadsheet may be a valuable tabulation of the verb tenses used in today's journals. Keep notes on how commonly the simple present tense occurs and also of any exceptions when the simple present tense is not the tense of choice. You will need this data especially after you finish writing your paper and are ready to edit it. Accomplished writers usually check the consistency of their verb tenses as the last step in polishing their manuscripts for publication. Remember not to pay attention to other language problems at the same time you check for tense consistency because, if you do, it will distract you from doing a thorough job.

Spreadsheet #5

This spreadsheet may contain helpful notes about the ways the articles you photocopied begin and how they end. Early and last sentences in articles are important. Check how these are written. When you finish writing your paper, turn to this spreadsheet again. You will compose a much better – a simpler and more direct – beginning after you have finished writing your paper than you will at any earlier point. Endings must be sensitively written for it is here that some authors make greater claims than their data support. Avoid doing this.

Spreadsheet #6

This spreadsheet has valuable information about giving credit to other research and other researchers. Study your articles carefully to see how, where, and when this is done. Your professional reputation in science may depend on the accuracy with which you give credit to others.

USING YOUR SPREADSHEETS

The spreadsheets are your model. Begin to use them by organizing the information on the spreadsheets in such a way that you can refer to them easily. Then as you begin writing you will keep an ongoing sheet of particular words or phrases about which you need more information. Perhaps you will make further spreadsheets, which will extend and complete your model for writing a successful scientific paper. Keep the spreadsheets. Use them. Modify them by adding new information and discarding data you find you no longer need.

Anytime you have a question about the written presentation of a certain idea, your spreadsheets should help you. If your spreadsheets are not sufficient help, a careful scan of a relevant published article written by a native speaker of English should provide what you need. Even writers who do not keep spreadsheets usually have their own personal lists of appealing words and phrases with notes of where they were found and how each was used.

> *If we knew what we were doing, it would not be called research.*
>
> *– Albert Einstein, 1879–1955*

YOUR FIRST DRAFT

The first draft can be written partially or completely in whatever language is easiest for you. It does not need to be written in English because the purpose of a first draft is to establish the skeleton, the bones, of your article. Your goal at this point is to get all your ideas down and, especially, to establish the sequence of ideas. While you are writing the first draft, whether it is in another language, partly in English, or completely in English, you should mark it with a private code which will help you write your next draft.

A Private Code

A private code involves putting personal annotations on the text as you write. Some writers do this by:

- Underlining words, phrases, and sentences.
- Using bold font.
- Leaving blank areas in the middle of sentences, or a series of symbols such as stars.
- Using symbols or words in another language.

Chapter 2

A private code is a sort of map of the thinking you do as you compose the first draft. It is your way of talking to yourself about what needs help without forcing you to slow down and fix it then. A private code permits you to continue writing down ideas even when you are aware the language is still incomplete.

Good writers have learned that pausing to look up words or checking data while they are writing slows their cognitive flow down and inhibits getting a clear sequence of ideas on paper. Further, good writers have found that when they write without marking a manuscript with a private code, they often mislead themselves into later thinking a piece of poor language is fine, and then they embarrass themselves by inadvertently carrying it on into a final draft.

Whatever code you invent, your intention is to mark places so that you can return to them easily when you write a second draft. Design a code that covers positives as well as negatives. The positives will mark places you felt confident about in your first draft, and knowledge of what you thought was good is as important as knowledge of places which need more work. Usually a private code is applied in computer symbols or fonts that are easily recognized later, but some writers print the draft first and then apply a private code in pencil or ink. Either way works as long as a map of the writer's thinking is provided which will aid the writer in the rewriting process.

So, invent your own private code. Keep it simple. Modify it a bit when you first use it but then stick with it. Memorize it. Write it down so you can't forget it between papers. Avoid changing your code drastically or changing your system between manuscripts. Changes may then cause your private code to end up confusing you more than helping you.

Organizing the Sequence of Your Ideas

The sequence in which you present your ideas is basic to the success of your paper. Attempt to get the sequence established before you begin the actual writing of the paper. This sounds easier than it is. Organizing a clear, lucid sequence can be difficult because in scientific research a number of things appear to need to be told simultaneously. Since they cannot be told simultaneously, this is beyond doubt the most difficult part of writing a first draft and one that needs to be solved before you start to write. If you do not get it solved, you may commit the worst possible crime in writing a research report which you hope to get published, namely your paper may contain repetition.

In order to accomplish a sequence which is clean, precise, and without repetition, you might consider using a pre-writing technique called 'story board' often used by newspaper reporters and detectives. In this technique, each idea is written separately on an index card, a piece of paper, or a post-it. Index cards are the most versatile: They can be arranged and rearranged in sequences as you search for the most logical order. They can be carried in a pocket and the logic be reevaluated until you can commit to a solid enough sequence to begin a first draft. When pieces of paper or post-its are used, they can be posted on a wall where you or you and a colleague or two can agree on a good sequence. At that point the cards or paper are numbered, and keywords can be written on them to help with the writing. You might even put each idea into a rudimentary sentence, but getting the sequence into sentences is not important yet. What is important is to organize a sound sequence in which ideas do not repeat and each event is in a logical order.

Chapter 2

Completing a First Draft

In the first draft you should put little effort into details such as getting vocabulary right, guarding against repeated language, checking tenses, evaluating transitions. Instead, whenever you fear you may not be making a good choice, use your private code to mark the place, and move on. At this point you should not be interested in polished language. You have now completed a first draft. It is far from a finished manuscript but it is an accomplishment of which you should be proud. Take a break of several hours or overnight before beginning a second draft. You need to give your mind a rest and chance to gain perspective, yet not give yourself so long that you will have forgotten the thinking you did during your first draft.

Four problems in manuscripts have caused innumerable papers to be rejected. Before you go beyond your first draft, check your plans against these deadly sins:

- The scope of the manuscript is too broad; this material should be divided into 2–3 papers and resubmitted.
- The claim of this manuscript goes beyond the given data.
- The manuscript is too lengthy, includes unnecessary details such as an overly long review of history, or redundancy.
- The authors have failed to give appropriate credit to others.

THE NEXT DRAFTS

In your first draft you established the sequence of ideas and events. Now, determine where you should use paragraphing to help the reader understand the divisions of your sequence.

Next, check all the places in your first draft where you used your private code. Replace all non-English words and refine the problems. Begin to turn to your spreadsheets for help. Work with them in whatever order you prefer, checking carefully through your manuscript with each spreadsheet and rewriting as you go.

> *Once more unto the breach, dear friends, once more;*
> *— Shakespeare*
> *Henry V*
> *Act III, scene i*

Even a highly skilled writer, who is a native speaker of English, does not write a successful paper in a single draft. All successful articles undergo a number of drafts before they are ready to be sent to journals. In each draft you will continue looking back at the information you have on your spreadsheets, checking, rechecking, and rewriting. Possibly your spreadsheets will not contain enough information and you will need to turn back to the articles you photocopied for further help.

In all these next drafts, most of your attention will be on transposing your entire first draft into simple, straightforward, English sentences. Keep sentences short and direct. A wise Australian journal editor once said a complicated sentence is like a stressed molecule. So, resist all temptation to try for long or beautiful sentences: You can lengthen sentences later; you can add grace later; you can combine ideas and add transitions to smooth out the meaning later. It is vital to keep your ideas direct and simple. Remember scientists all over the world are eager to be able to understand what you report; help them out. Speak to them simply and directly, scientist to scientist.

Chapter 2

Do not worry at this point that what you have written may sound simplistic. On one level, you want your writing to be simplistic because being simplistic means being clear and you want everyone to be able to understand what you have written. As you continue on to the intensive editing in your final draft you will get variety in the choices of vocabulary, transitions, and sentence structure so that your article sounds smoother and more interesting. Your main goal will be to ensure that the ideas in each sentence:

- would be clear to any other scientist in your field,
- are referenced properly wherever credit should be given to others,
- do not bore the reader with historic or other types of details that are not directly related to the topic of your article, and
- do not insult the intelligence of your readers by over-explaining the obvious.

YOUR FINAL DRAFT

Now, at last it is time to create the final draft in which you edit your manuscript, to make it as good as you have dreamed it could be. You are ready to practice the art of editing.

> *To unpathed waters, undreamed shores.*
> *– Shakespeare*
> *Winters Tale*
> *Act IV, scene iv*

– 3 –

The Art of Editing What You Write

"Without editors, writers are nothing but makers of lace."
– C. Shields (2003) Unless, Random
House of Canada, 177

Who will help you edit? Certainly not editors of scientific journals: Editorial staffs of journals do not provide this service. They will return your paper, often after only reading enough to see that the style of language you have used does not fit that of their journal. If you get any advice, beyond a simple rejection, from the journal to which you send your paper, it will probably be a sentence telling you to get language help for your paper.

How does this affect you and what can you do? First of all, many amateur or unpublished writers take their writing far too personally. Whatever is said about their writing they take to apply to them as a person – as a scientist. Don't do this, for if you react this way, you may never get a paper in good enough shape to be published. The quality of your writing does not reflect on your intelligence or your worth as a scientist, only on one of your skills.

> *Now is the winter of our discontent . . .*
> *– Shakespeare*
> *Richard III*
> *Act I, scene i*

Second, as a writer of science you need to realize that what you write is a product: A product similar to a cake a baker mixes together and bakes. The success of the cake depends on the quality of the ingredients, the quantity of the ingredients, the sequence of putting them together, and a tender touch. When the cake turns out well, we congratulate the baker. However, when the cake does not turn out well, we do not think badly of the baker as a person, only as a baker of cake. To get a manuscript published you must learn to edit your manuscript several times with colleagues, and do it carefully, or else stop – so to speak – trying to make a cake.

Third, remember that writing is a social activity. Even when you write alone, writing is a social activity, because you are always writing for an audience of readers, seeking their understanding. You need others to reassure you that your manuscript is written so that all readers will understand each of your points.

FINDING EDITING HELP

Where should you go to get editing help? Professional editors who are not scientists and are unfamiliar with your type of science can be extremely undependable in their choice of improvements. Their ability to edit the kind of English used in newspaper reporting, essays, novels, and personal letters may be excellent, but they are not knowledgeable about the way language is used to report research in science journals. Other services devoted only to science are often of little better help because even they often lack specific knowledge of your particular field. So beware, and, if you choose to use a professional editing service, wherever there is a disagreement between what the service suggests and what your spreadsheets tell you, trust the spreadsheets. [See Chapter 2 for information about spreadsheets.]

You will need help in order to edit your paper well. Few successful writers of science edit alone. In fact few of them even write alone. They write in teams and edit for each other. No one writes or edits well enough to work alone: The English language is too slippery. You need other eyes and minds to help you. Most scientists edit with a colleague; some with two colleagues although working with more than two others can create more chaos than help.

> *I will wear my heart upon my sleeve for daws to peck at.*
>
> *— Shakespeare*
> *Othello*
> *Act I, scene i*

You need to make a careful choice of the person, or people, with whom you write or edit. You must know and trust each so well that you will not take their comments and questions personally, keeping foremost in your mind that all suggestions are meant kindly and intended to improve the clarity of the science. In turn, the person or people who work with you must trust you: They must believe that you will not be personally offended by their suggestions.

You will be wisest to set up such a confidential editing system with someone who is your peer, not someone who is your superior, or someone who works under you. Ideally you will find a peer or peers also writing papers so that you can form a team of writers who edit for each other. Computers now allow us to write and edit with peers in other institutions, which opens up more possibilities for collaboration and good editing than ever before.

Attempt to meet with your other colleagues at conferences or for coffee at their institution because friendship is an important part of maintaining the openness and trust required for editing to be successful and completed in a timely fashion. Remember you can only be helped by someone who:

- trusts you to be open to both positive and negative criticism,
- is capable of giving both positive as well as negative criticism,
- knows your work well, and
- is familiar with the type of writing in the journal in which you plan to publish.

A team of people to write and edit with may be hard to find and coming to a workable agreement with them will require both personal and professional effort. However, writing is too social an activity for us to be able to receive the kind of help we need, and the kind we can understand, from people who do not know us or our research.

Chapter 3

ELIMINATING UNNECESSARY LANGUAGE

English in itself, due to its grammar, is a redundant language and writers who want to be respected as well as to show respect to their readers, make every effort to avoid all unnecessary language. This means you must edit out any words, sentences, and phrases that are not essential to meaning.

Repetition & Redundancy

Editors tell us that repetition (directly repeating the same words) and redundancy (indirect repetition through alternate phrases or synonyms) are common flaws in rejected papers and that these are particularly common in the writing of scientists whose native language is not English. Unfortunately repetition is even less tolerated in science journals than it was years ago. It is understandable that repetition is a language trap easy to fall into because English has a richness of synonyms plus almost endless varieties of syntactical structures for expressing identical thoughts. Therefore writers can easily convince themselves that they are not repeating but merely emphasizing points and making them clearer. However editors have quick eyes for all forms of repetition and they don't respect any of them.

31

You get to make a point once and only once. You can make it clearly and powerfully by your careful choice of succinct language, but you only get to say it once. Ideas, no matter how important, how complicated, or how innovative, are not restated or rephrased within the body of a research article. The only acceptable repetition occurs in a final summary where vital information can be briefly restated without detailed explanation.

> *Most writing, untouched by editing, is banal and repetitive.*
> *— A. Eisenberg, Scientific American,*
> *December 2001, p. 97*

Repeated Vocabulary

Repetition of the same non-science vocabulary, especially verbs, will make your manuscript dull. Replace some repeated non-technical words with alternate words that will mean the same and often be more accurate. Do this for all non-science vocabulary by setting your computer to scan your article to show how often you have repeated an interest-adding word or phrase.

Note that a thesaurus is a dangerous source for finding an alternate word to use. English is both too subtle and too complex for a thesaurus to be a safe tool. Your only reliable information is in your spreadsheets and the articles you photocopied. If neither of these contain the vocabulary you seek, find other recent articles written by native English speakers, photocopy them, and add data from them to your spreadsheets.

A final warning: After you have seasoned your manuscript with more interesting language take care that you haven't used a particularly eye-catching word or phrase more than once. Such words or phrases add spice to your writing, which is good, but they stand out prominently. So set your computer to find each of these. Choose the most effective place for each, and use each only once.

Unnecessary Explanation or Description

An important form of unnecessary language in a research article is the presence of additional information, which is interesting and fun to write but which is irrelevant to the results being reported. Through a careful use of your spread-sheets, you may have already eliminated this type of lengthy explanation, but, if not, you need to scan again to be certain your manuscript has avoided using:

- More background or history than the journal to which you plan to send normally prints.
- Too many details about what was done – or even worse, details about unsuccessful work.
- Information about other research your group has done.

> *Things should always be made as simple as possible and no simpler*
> *— Albert Einstein, 1879–1955*

Prepositional Phrases
Another common form of unnecessary explanation lies in the overuse of qualifying prepositional phrases, such as writing 'in our laboratory', when where the work has taken place is

obvious to the reader. Watch for extraneous information in prepositional phrases such as: 'by the researcher', 'during the research', 'on the table', 'in this group'. Remove all these irrelevant phrases as you edit. Note how few of these you were able to collect on the spreadsheets from your photocopied articles.

PASSIVE VOICE

Contemporary writing in science has become more and more direct and, as it has, the use of passive voice has been fast disappearing. Check your spreadsheets, or go back to the photocopied articles, to discover if you find verbs in passive voice. Change any you find to active voice, for examples see Table 2. The journals esteem active voice and direct statements.

You will want to check your final draft for sentences which begin:

- There are . . .
- There is . . .
- There was . . .
- There were . . .
- There has been . . .
- There have been . . .

Also check for all sentences that start with the word 'It' when 'It' is used without a referent as a generality:

- It was . . .
- It is . . .
- It has been . . .

Chapter 3

Passive structures are easy, familiar structures to use, and they will probably aid your ability to compose freely, so use them in your early drafts. However change them when you edit so that the content of each sentence is more quickly available to the reader. Moving directly to what you have to say creates a stronger paper and one more likely to be published. [For examples of how to rewrite 'It' sentences see Table 3.1]

Table 3.1 Examples of Indirect or Unnecessary Language from Unpublished Papers

Indirect language	Direct, clear language
It will be the end of the year before we **can** expect results **to be ready**.	We expect results by the end of the year.
It was discovered **in our laboratories** that sulfur dichloride reacts with . . .	We discovered sulfur dichloride reacts with . . .
It is vital to recognize **the importance of the** variance among lengths of multiple bonds.	Recognizing variance in the length of multiple bonds is vital.
It is very important **to realize** that the **aforementioned** results are . . .	The results are important because . . .
If my group **had been able to**, we **would have** prepared the compound but . . .	We have not prepared the compound because . . .
There have been recent developments in NMR which allow . . .	Recent developments in NMR allow . . .
There are three molecular orbitals, **namely**, 1) . . . 2) . . . , 3) . . .	The three molecular orbitals are: 1) . . . , 2) . . . , 3) . . .

EMPHASIZING MEANING WITH INTENSIFIERS

The impact of messages becomes stronger when writers avoid the addition of intensifiers, such as 'really', 'actually', 'truly'. These words add an almost slippery flavor to a research report. Such words belong in narrative writing, and a reader who finds them in science may withdraw in suspicion. Check your photocopied articles to see if these words ever appear. The best advice is to eliminate them in your final edit. They are good words to use socially, and are fine even in professional letters, but they do not belong in research reports. Strange as it may sound, your scientific statements are stronger when you omit these ambiguous intensifiers.

The Word 'Very'

'Very' is another word everyone should avoid. It is not ambiguous as an intensifier, but it has become so trite that it is basically meaningless. 'Very' is so common that your writing is stronger if you omit it. You can consider using intensifiers that are more effective at adding emphasis, such as 'extremely', 'highly', 'strongly', 'surprisingly', but use all intensifiers infrequently or they will lose their power and sound unscientific.

Other Overused Words

Free your manuscript from other overused words which reduce the intensity of your message. Replace words such as 'a lot' and 'many' with more specific meaningful words. You are a scientist; you can find specific words.

Also improve the impact of your words by omitting those that are not only overused but judgmental, such as 'good' or 'nice'. Avoid words that praise instead of explain: Good science explains not praises.

Exclamation Marks

Exclamation marks are seldom if ever seen in professional writing and certainly not in research reports. Instead you must make your emphasis clear by a careful choice of vocabulary. Some languages use exclamation marks in their scientific writing. English does not.

Remember if you leave an exclamation mark in, the journal will delete it so do them a favor and delete it yourself. Again, check your spreadsheet and photocopied articles to note that they do not contain exclamation marks.

CLICHÉS

Beware of clichés. Clichés are over-used idioms and using them is not respected in English. Although such phrases may seem to be colorful and certainly offer a seductive temptation to sound like a native English speaker, don't use them. They are considerably less effective than the simple direct words for which they stand.

Clichés in many languages are helpful, and in some languages preferred, but in English they are words once considered original and now regarded as trite. Clichés, in a language as dynamic and changing as English, quickly become so dated that reading them distracts people or, worse, invites them to laugh.

Familiar idioms which are so familiar as to have become clichés are of some value in informal conversation but not in scientific writing. Even in conversation, repetition of familiar descriptive phrases is not particularly respected or considered courteous. English speakers become slightly embarrassed for a speaker, and especially for a writer, who uses an overly familiar, out-of-date, descriptive phrase. Such phrases can seem slightly childish and the user may be thought to lack sophistication. Clichés are not appropriate in research reports. Table 3.2 displays some clichés from unpublished papers: The clichés are underlined.

WIT

Do not confuse clichés and wit. Scholarly wit is highly valued in good scientific writing. However, using wit successfully requires a superb knowledge of the English language. Successful wit in a science article is accomplished through an avoidance of redundancy and a lively choice of words.

The short length and requirements of research articles seldom afford room for wit even in the hands of an expert. Unfortunately wit is culturally dependent, which in this case means achieving a successful combination of the culture of science and the culture of the English language. This is difficult indeed.

**Table 3.2   Examples of Inappropriate Clichés and
Unnecessary Words from Unpublished Papers**

Inappropriate	Appropriate
Attempting **to do** this was **like trying to put a square peg in a round hole** . . .	Attempting this was difficult because . . .
In high hopes we **studied** the spectrometer printout and found . . .	Results of the spectrometer reading indicate . . .
Darwin's **tried and true** method of . . .	Darwin's method of . . .
We believe that **sooner or later** these results will . . .	We believe that these results will . . .
We are pleased to be able to report that the structure . . .	The structure is . . .
The findings **of the results of the study** show . . . **that** the end product **has** indicated . . .	The end product indicates . . .
The product is **black as coal** . . .	The product is an intense black color.
This result is **the cherry on top**.	This result adds to the evidence that . . .
This result is **beyond our wildest dreams**.	This result encourages us that . . .

TRANSITIONS

Transitional words and phrases are valuable within and between sentences. However overuse of any of them will weaken your final draft. Use as many of them as you want in your early drafts. In early drafts these are an aid to you because they tend to tighten up and guide your thinking. However in the final draft you need to check carefully to see:

- How many you have used; and
- Whether or not you have used them in places where the meaning requires them.

> *An honest tale speeds best being plainly told*
> *– Shakespeare*
> *Richard III*
> *Act IV, scene iv*

'Smoothers'

Some transitional words or phrases function as smoothers: They smooth the way between sentences in which the logic flows in an expected direction. Although a transition word or phrase is not required when the meaning continues on as expected, a judicious use of such optional transitions smoothes readers' ability to follow along as your writing moves from idea to idea. Use of optional transitions is easy and natural for most writers. However, overuse of smoothers will weaken your writing and distract your readers. Check your photocopied articles for how often successful authors use them. [Figure 3.1.]

'Contradictors'

On the other hand help from transitional words or phrases is usually required when a sentence or paragraph contradicts

- furthermore
- in addition
- first, second, third, etc. (archaic: firstly, secondly, thirdly etc.)
- finally
- lastly
- moreover
- incidentally
- in fact
- in truth
- as a matter of fact
- for example
- such as
- next
- then

**Figure 3.1   'Smoothers': Transitions that Continue an
Expected Flow of Logic**

- but
- however
- instead
- nevertheless
- despite
- surprisingly
- in spite of
- in contrast
- for comparison

**Figure 3.2   'Contradictors': Transitions that Indicate
Change to an Expected Flow of Logic**

the on-going logic of the previous idea. These transition words or phrases are seldom optional. [See Figure 3.2.] They serve to warn the reader that the direction of the logic is about to change.

'Explainers'

Explainers are transitions used to show cause and effect. These transitions are sometimes optional and often occur in the middle of sentences. They are especially valuable to signal that you are giving results or conclusions. [Figure 3.3.]

Guidelines for Editing Transitions

Three general guidelines can help you when you edit your use of transitions:

- If a current reputable journal article written by an English speaker uses the term, it is probably a good choice.
- The role of transition words or phrases is to clarify the meaning to readers. This is their only role.
- Using transitions more than 10–12 times on a full page of text is apt to interfere with, not help, the readers' comprehension.

  - because
  - as a result
  - therefore
  - in general
  - consequently
  - as predicted
  - in conclusion
  - since
  - as
  - for
  - finally

Figure 3.3   'Explainers': Transitions that Indicate Cause and Effect

Chapter 3

Dated transitions

Transitions that have gone out-of-date include phrases such as 'as was mentioned earlier', 'the aforementioned', 'the authors would like to say' and any other phrases that remind an otherwise intelligent reader that the content has already been stated, or will be stated later. In current thinking, these old-fashioned phrases mildly insult the reader and interfere with comprehension. They should not be used.

EDITING VERB TENSES

The final and most tedious edit is to examine each verb tense in the paper for agreement and consistency. This should be done after all other revisions and edits have been made. While you are conducting this final tense check, do not let yourself pause to consider anything else in the manuscript. Even teachers of English easily overlook inconsistencies in tense when they let their concentration stray while they are doing a tense check.

Present Tenses

Simple Present Tense
The most common tense in scientific writing today is the simple present tense. All results, whether done today or years ago, are referred to in present tense. The implication of this use of the simple present tense is that the finding is an all-time truth, which would occur again were the experiment

repeated. In contrast, using the past tense for a research result may imply the finding is no longer true.

Check your spreadsheets and photocopied articles to discover when, or if, a verb is used in any form other than the simple present tense. Add these examples to your spreadsheets along with the apparent reason for the unusual tense. Decide to make the simple present tense your friend.

> *If at first, you don't succeed, try, try again*
> *– German proverb*

Present Progressive Tense
Non-English speakers should be especially suspicious of being a friend of the present progressive tense, i.e. forms of the verb 'to be' followed by a verb plus '–ing'. Foreign speakers of English tend to use this tense far more than native speakers of English. Progressive tenses are fine in conversation, narrative writing, and letters, but they are seldom found in professional or scientific writing. Reserve the present progressive tense for those highly unusual times when you must emphasize the event is in progress right now. [Tables 1 & 3.]

Present Perfect Tenses
Present perfect tenses can be not only correct but quite elegant in research reporting. However the perfect tenses are seldom required, and they do require more language knowledge than the simpler tenses. [Tables 3.1 & 3.3.]

Chapter 3

Past Tenses

Past tenses are also commonly used in scientific writing, but only under certain circumstances.

Simple Past Tense
Present past tense is used to refer to what was done during laboratory work. Within a research article, the use of simple past tense to explain procedures is usually the only exception to the use of simple present tense. Other uses are no longer common and you should check your spreadsheets and photocopied articles for more information. [Table 3.3.]

Past Perfect Tenses
Past perfect tenses can also be appropriate, but the simple past tense is safer and often better.

Table 3.3   Examples of Inappropriate Tenses from Unpublished Papers

Inappropriate Tense	Tense Preferred in Science
Sodium **is reacting** with water.	Sodium **reacts** with water
Sodium **reacted** with water	Sodium **reacts** with water
The results **are showing** that . . .	The results **show** that . . .
Results **showed** that . . .	Results **show** that . . .
Our group **has been proposing** that . . .	We **propose** that . . .
Some researchers **are arguing** that . . .	Some researchers **argue** that . . .

Past Progressive Tense

Check your spreadsheets and photocopied articles in case you can find an example of this being used well in a recent science article written by a native English speaker. They are rare and usually unnecessary.

THE VOICE OF SCIENCE

Congratulations, you have polished the language of your manuscript. Your paper is a clarion call to scientists like yourself: You have modified sentences, evaluated the use of transitions, eliminated excess language, improved vocabulary, and checked the consistency of tenses. Your readers can now rely on the accuracy of your words because you have made your message clear to all the innocent scientists of the world who were not in the lab with you.

- You have remembered that writers forget their audiences at their peril.
- Your manuscript now speaks in the voice of science.

> *Good science is not written. It is rewritten.*
> *– R. West, 1928–*

– 4 –

The Art of Dancing with Change

---

*"English is destined to be in the next and
succeeding centuries more generally the language
of the world than Latin was in the last or French is
in the present age. The reason of this is obvious,
because the increasing population in America, and
their universal connection and correspondence
with all nations will, aided by the influence of
England in the world, whether great or small, force
their language into general use."*
– John Adams, American colonies, 1780

Most native speakers of English consider they speak and write 'standard English', or 'the Queen's English', or at least 'good English'. However, even Welsh linguist, David Crystal, the world's most respected living authority on the English language, says 'standard English', the 'Queen's English', and 'good English' do not exist: Not in dictionaries, not in books, not in people's mouths. Instead we all speak and write with regional differences. Each of these different dialogues are labeled by those who are educated and live in English-speaking countries as 'standard English', or 'the Queen's

English', and, above all, 'good English'. The various species of English-speaking fish have always swum in such murky waters that it has never been possible to catch one and declare, 'This is a proper fish.'

At present North American English seems to prevail over British English in international communication. Probably this has occurred due to economic and technological advantages, but it may be simply due to numbers. The population of the United States is four to five times the population of the United Kingdom, so on that basis alone we could expect more language innovation from the American side. In the near future, more people will be communicating internationally in English than the population of North America and the United Kingdom combined. If number of users affects language change, we may be about to experience extremely rapid change as English-language fish from many other cultures swim in the river.

TRENDS IN INTERNATIONAL ENGLISH

Ever since the advent of the World Wide Web, societies have reeled under the impact of needing to communicate rapidly and effectively with other countries. In the world-wide effort to improve communication, we have only begun to establish what may become known as international English. A Cherokee chief in the 1800s called English the language of deception. To whatever degree this was, or is, true of English, it is not a valuable characteristic in science.

Scientists around the world desire to use language in order to give and receive information without ambiguous nuances. Scientists will welcome changes that result in a more international, clearer English, because in no other field is a direct and simple international language so needed as it is in science.

Disappearing Differences between British English and North American English

In the process of becoming a world language, differences between British and North American English are fast disappearing. Some differences in lexicon exist: 'lorry'/'truck', 'torch'/'flashlight', 'boot'/'trunk', 'pudding'/'dessert', 'pram'/'baby buggy', 'nappy'/'diaper', 'sweet'/'candy', 'biscuit'/'cookie', and 'wallet'/'billfold', but none of these are words that appear commonly in science.

Few, if any, differences in grammar are found any more. Spelling differences are still noticeable, but even these are fast fading under the influence of the Internet.

> *In days of old, when*
> *Knights were bold,*
> *And science not*
> *Invented. The Earth*
> *Was flat, And that*
> *Was that, with no*
> *One discontented.*
>
> *— anonymous, 1800s*

Spelling

North American spelling has become more common than British among the majority of the world's English-language users. A glance at the journal you plan to submit an article to will show you which spelling the journal prefers. Which you choose is unimportant as long as you are consistent. A journal will not reject your manuscript because you use British not North American spelling, or vice versa.

Table 4.1 shows some remaining differences in spelling although these are of little concern anymore as word-processing programs easily locate and make the changes for us.

Style

The style of British English is more formal than North American English. The differences in style are of little concern to the readers of this book as they are rarely apparent in a well-written science paper. However, differences in style may affect the wording you choose for narrative writing in cover letters, introductory letters, and correspondence between colleagues. [See Chapter 5 for examples of letters.]

American English makes less use of polite, ambiguous verb forms, such as: 'could', 'would', 'should', 'might', 'can', 'may'. These auxiliary verbs can be extremely slippery: Sometimes some are interchangeable; other times they are not. At any rate, they are apt to convey meanings different from what the writer intends; their meanings are subtle and dependent on context. One use of such words has been to add grace to personal correspondence or cover letters, but this kind of use requires a high sensitivity to the English language as well as to what is appropriate. When in doubt, resolve your debate by replacing the verbs accompanied by auxiliaries with their simpler verb forms.

**Table 4.1   Some Spelling Differences between British
and North American English**

British	North American
• advertize, advertizement	• advertise, advertisement
• aluminium	• aluminum
• analogue, catalogue, dialogue	• analog, catalog, dialog
• cancelled, cancelling	• canceled, canceling
• centre	• center
• cheque	• check
• colour, honour, labour, valour, humour	• color, honor, labor, valor, humor
• favour, favourable	• favor, favorable
• focussed, focussing	• focused, focusing
• gaol	• jail
• enquiry	• inquiry
• inflexion	• inflection
• jewellery	• jewelry
• licence	• license
• litre	• liter
• practise	• practice
• manoeuvre	• maneuver
• neighbour	• neighbor
• organise	• organize
• sceptical	• skeptical
• specialise	• specialize
• sulphur	• sulfur
• theatre	• theater
• travelled, travelling	• traveled, traveling
• tyre	• tire
• vigour	• vigor

Personal correspondence in American English tends to be more informal than British English. For example, especially in American English, the words 'whom' and 'shall' are often replaced with 'who' and 'will', the difference between 'among' and 'between' is often ignored, and the subjunctive can be found without its traditional reversal of verb–subject agreement. How far this trend will go is unknown but it does serve to simplify grammar.

The current style of North American English in personal letters often seems breezy or even impolite. Create spreadsheets from the letters you receive, which can guide you in the style you choose to use. Notice that North American English tends to contain new idioms. These sometimes seem appealing, but they go out-of-date or change meaning so rapidly that they are not helpful: Avoid them. Writers are safest who resist the temptation to write as informally as some Americans do.

Changing Places of Parts of Speech

Traditionally we all like a grammar that can be learned, can be depended upon. This is not how English is. One of its more frustrating characteristics must be the freedom it seems to have to take one part of speech and use it as another. However, this is also one of the glories of English. It has more flexibility than any other language because its syntax easily adapts to new content and allows it to take in new ideas.

Nouns Becoming Verbs/Nouns Becoming Adjectives
Nouns today sometimes change from nouns, to verbs, to adjectives without even changing their form. For example

52

we can get email; email someone; and get email letters. We can work in an office; office with someone; use office supplies. No other language has this – what some consider scandalous – flexibility. When you see an example of these trends in a science article, look it up in a dictionary published 2000 CE or later. If it is there, add it to your spreadsheets.

Adjectives Being Used as Adverbs
Americans have a tendency to use adjective forms in place of adverbs. The use of 'good' in situations where 'well' has been traditional, 'different' for 'differently', or 'slow' instead of 'slowly'. How common or accepted this will be in the future is unknown. So far they are not considered to be correct usage.

Moving Toward Faster and More Direct Communication

International English seems to be moving toward faster and more direct communication. Many of us may find new trends an annoying use of language even though they get meaning across quickly. An important part of this trend in science journals is the use of active voice instead of passive voice along with the use of simple present tense, both in the name of getting messages across directly and quickly. See, for example, if you agree that the active-voice, present tense sentences in the right column of Table 3.2 are easier and faster to comprehend than the passive-voice, progressive tense sentences in the left column.

Punctuation

Contemporary English uses less punctuation than was traditionally used. How much internal punctuation is required in sentences is changing, so, when in doubt, check your spreadsheets and photocopied articles. The direction of change, however, is toward simplicity.

Capital Letters

English has been dropping capital letters for over a hundred years. Early in the 1900s abstract qualities such as 'love', 'nature', 'strength', 'loyalty', and 'beauty' were no longer honored by being capitalized. Soon after the seasons, 'winter', 'spring', 'summer', 'fall', lost their capital letters. Then words such as 'university', 'professor', 'doctor', 'chemistry' lost their capitals, except when used in titles, 'Kyoto University', 'Professor Dreiss', 'Dr. Lee', 'Chemistry Department'.

We can only guess which capitals will next become considered unnecessary and disappear. One can only be amazed at the singular egotism with which English capitalizes the pronoun 'I' and yet does not give this respect to any other of the personal pronouns – surely embarrassment will eventually put an end to referring to oneself as "I".

Rarely is a new discovery or technological event so astonishing that it gets gifted with a capital as did the Internet: There was a phenomenon worthy of an "I"! Although the Internet retains its capital in early 2000 CE dictionaries, if trends in capitalization continue, then soon we should see 'internet' without the capital. Similarly, the preferred punctuation of 'World Wide Web' may soon be 'world wide web'.

54

Chapter 4

Hyphens
The modern trend is to eliminate hyphens except when using two words to form an adjective: 'English-speaking person', 'panic-stricken person'. Old friends such as 'co-operation'/'re-unification' have become 'cooperation'/ 'reunification', and even words originally considered too odd looking or hard to pronounce, such as 'reestablish', have become correct form. The modern trend is to combine old forms into single words.

Commas
The trend has been to use fewer and fewer commas. Today a comma is required only when a clause or phrase is not in its expected place in a sentence and to separate items in a series. Most writers of science have now agreed to place a comma before 'and' in a series.

Acronyms and Abbreviations
The English language, especially in science, has moved rapidly to the acceptance of acronyms and abbreviations. This seems to be part of the move toward quicker recognition and faster comprehension. Note that the brain comprehends at a far greater speed than eyes can move over print.

Until relatively recently acronyms included the use of periods after each letter. Use of a period (full stops/dot) after each letter first became optional and now has disappeared. Instead acronyms are now correctly spelled in capital letters, without further punctuation: RSVP, UK, CIM, RAM, ROM, USA, ASAP, TV.

Abbreviations today, especially in science, are an odd mixture of correct styles. Abbreviations for single words are spelled with an ending period, for example: Dr. Abdul, Prof. Leites, no. (number), fig. (figure). Yet units of measure have no capitals and the ending period vanishes, as in: kg (kilogram), cm (centimeter), km (kilometer).

Then some units of measure are acronyms and in these the ending periods as well as the capital letters disappear, as in: ppm (parts per million), rpm (revolutions per minute), kph (kilometers per hour), bps (bits per second). Interestingly enough symbols named for people still usually take capitals: N (Newton), K (Kelvin), T (Torr, from Torricelli).

For a complete list of acceptable short forms for terms used in the sciences refer to *Elsevier's Dictionary of Acronyms, Initialisms, Abbreviations, and Symbols* (2003).

Emoticons

At the extreme and unhelpful end of the tendency to shorter ways to communicate in English are 'emoticons'. This is an intriguingly new and still evolving linguistic trend which tends to delight, annoy, or puzzle us in the emails we receive.

Possibly you have seen graphics showing emoticons as they are symbols which can be found displayed in dictionaries published since 2000 CE. 'Emoticon', a word formed by blend of the words 'emotion' and 'icon' is an arrangement of keyboard characters, which are intended to be viewed sideways as symbolic pictures conveying emotions, for example, 'faces' that look happy, sad, shocked, bored, or scared. None of these are in common use and at this time do not belong in professional correspondence.

The list of such oddities has been further expanded to include acronyms for a large number of phases: 'CUS' for 'see you soon' or 'IMHO' for 'in my humble opinion'. These are of even less value and less understood than emoticons and highly unlikely to be helpful or amusing outside an extremely small circle of friends. Please do not use them in international communication.

Keep sensitive to changes that occur in the Internet correspondence you receive, evaluate who the author is, and choose the models you follow with care. Some styles are at present overly casual and you should be hesitant about imitating them. However, stay alert because what is acceptable is changing all the time.

> *Double, double toil and trouble; Fire burn and*
> *cauldron bubble.*
> *— Shakespeare*
> *MacBeth*
> *Act IV, scene i*

Questions

Avoid asking questions of the reader in your paper. This technique has gone out of fashion and is seldom seen. Instead you are expected to make statements that give readers information. It is considered a bit autocratic and controlling to ask questions of people who are not there to answer.

Check your spreadsheets and photocopied articles. Perhaps you will be able to find an article in which a question is posed to the reader. However, these are rare and the most you will ever find in an international journal is one per article. So, discipline yourself to make careful statements instead and save your questions for times when you address a live audience that has, at least the possibility, of answering.

The Mysterious Word 'The'

Perhaps international change will be able to destroy the grounds for the myth that correct use of the word 'the' can only be understood by native speakers of English. However, today this word is used by native speakers of English with less consistency and more mystery than most non-native speakers want to tolerate. The articles 'a' and 'an' are easy to use correctly compared to the mysterious and rather noble-sounding 'the'.

A frustrating aspect of understanding the use of 'the' is that children born to English-speaking parents have no difficulty with it by the time they enter school. Consequently, instruction is not given to them, nor is there sufficiently helpful instruction in grammar books. So we all leave school believing that the frequent and often beautiful use of 'the' in stories, newspapers, and poetry is the way to use 'the'. And then some of us become scientists and want to write in the style of science journals.

The style of writing in scientific journals, especially in research reports, uses fewer 'the's than any other forms of writing. Many 'the's in English are optional, and science, luckily for you, takes the opportunity to omit as many optional ones as possible. In science today, this is somewhat of a problem for native as well as non-native English writers, but native speakers have 'an ear' for whether or not it can be left out and whether or not it should be left in. Probably you will need years to develop 'an ear', and the good advice of 'When in doubt, leave it out' may get you into trouble. Your most helpful source will be found in the spreadsheet information you gather from recent journal articles.

USING A DATABASE PUBLISHED AFTER 2000 CE

The final step in the art of dancing with language change is to use the music of a recent dictionary to accompany you. The early part of this new century has seen English adding words and altering word meanings at an unprecedented rate. Further, linguists predict this rate of change will increase as English continues to expand into a global language in an international world.

Writers of science must realize the value of checking on the age of their language database, whether in a book or on a computer. Many of the spell-check programs in use today fail to recognize changes in language which have been in place for years. Dictionaries on CD-ROM or on our desks are misleading if they are more than a few years old. Certainly those published before 2000 CE are no longer sufficiently helpful.

Whichever British or American database you choose, you will find each has a certain approach and priorities. For example, among the many American dictionaries, the *Random House Webster's College Dictionary* along with other Random House dictionaries are some of the few that, in addition to adding new words to each addition, attempt to put the most common meaning first. This is in contrast to dictionaries which prioritize meanings in less helpful ways, such as historical entrance into the language. Random House also lists new and old idioms by year of entry into the language, and so far has kept abreast of additions from the Internet and computers.

A relatively new dictionary, *Microsoft Encarta College Dictionary: The First Dictionary for the Internet Age* (2001), has a helpful unbiased emphasis on the language of current politics as well as on recent technology. However, it does this at the cost of omitting some of the historical and much of the etymological information in other dictionaries. An unabridged form of this dictionary was published in 2005.

Decide what is most important to you in a dictionary or database and choose yours accordingly. Finding out about the currency and usefulness of your language data base is essential. Scientists using old dictionaries continue to operate in danger zones.

A RECENT EXAMPLE OF LANGUAGE CHANGE

The evolution of the term used to refer to what we now call 'email' provides an interesting example of ongoing language change. The word has migrated through language changes demonstrating, in turn, the contemporary tendency to:

- adopt abbreviations,
- drop capital letters,

- omit hyphens,
- use nouns as verbs.

Even though the term for electronic mail was first used publicly 1975–1980, the 1984 edition of the *Random House dictionary* lists only 'electronic data processing' and 'electronic music' with no entry for 'electronic mail'. Then, as the practice of sending mail by computer became more common, the entry added a capital letter to create 'Electronic mail', as if to acknowledge its importance.

Then, following post-modern trends in English to drop capitals and accept abbreviations, the 1992 *Random House Dictionary* drops the capital 'E' and lists 'electronic mail', and includes as a separate entry, 'E-mail', interestingly enough giving the abbreviation a capital 'E'. However by 1997 the dictionary drops the 'E' and the entry becomes 'e-mail'. Finally following current trends to drop hyphens and form a single word, by 2001 even the conservative Oxford University Press' *Oxford Dictionary of Current English* lists 'email' as the correct spelling. Further dictionaries now list the word as a verb as well as a noun. Presumably this completes the evolution of the accepted term for electronic mail, giving us a fine example of how rapidly the English language is changing.

FUTURE OF THE ART OF DANCING WITH CHANGE

English by means of the World Wide Web is spreading into more and more corners of the world, expanding and revising itself through other languages, and gathering new riches. Although English appears to be the strongest horse in today's race to ride across the plains of the planet, all riders should sit firmly in their saddles and keep close eyes on the horizon. One German professor said recently that in science he now thinks better in English than in German. If this should become true of others around the world, we should all be concerned about what science may be losing. Surely science needs the insights that come through thinking in other languages, for these may be the insights that change and expand the nature of science.

> *All people in this world are one of three types: those who are immovable, those who may be moved, and those who move.*
> *— Arab proverb*

– 5 –

The Art of Writing Abstracts, Proposals, and Letters

A vital piece in having an article accepted for publication in an international journal, of being accepted as a speaker at an international conference, or of writing a successful grant is your ability to write good abstracts, clear proposals, and appropriate letters. None of these are difficult but they all require special skills.

> *Brevity is the soul of wit.*
>
> *– Shakespeare*
> *Hamlet*
> *Act II, scene ii*

ABSTRACTS

Every journal and every conference will expect your research paper or proposal to be accompanied by an abstract. The abstract will be read first, and its quick clarity will strongly influence whether or not your work is further considered for publication or for presentation. The abstract is designed to tell a scientific story that is easily understood and can, in turn, be quickly conveyed to others.

An abstract is an extract of the essence of your work. Abstracts are not summaries; they are more concise and clearer than summaries. Summaries are often organized chronologically; abstracts are not. Abstracts are built around importance. They give what was discovered, how it was done, how it fits with other research, and what it suggests for future research. They are an exercise in precise, accurate language.

The difficulty in writing an abstract is that the abstract must be short – indeed very short. Most journals' instructions tell authors to send in abstracts of as few as 100 words or less. Conference abstracts sometimes require as few as 50 words. Writing a good abstract requires extreme discipline even from those who normally are superb writers of English.

Writing an abstract requires unusual cognitive and linguistic discipline. Excess words must be carefully eliminated until the ones that remain ring true to fellow scientists' brains and to English-speaking ears. The clarity of the words will determine: First, whether others will read your work, and, second and perhaps even more important, if readers will accurately report its information to others.

One well-published chemist at the University of Wisconsin proudly states that he can write a shorter abstract than anyone else. If so, he is appreciated by all journal editors, readers, and organizers of conferences. The five maxims for writing abstracts are:

- Stay within or under the required number of words.
- Edit carefully.
- Have a colleague who knows your work well edit.
- Edit again.
- Check your word choices and structures against other recent abstracts in the journal to which you plan to send your paper, or against previous proceedings of the conference to which you are applying.

Your abstract will be read by far more people than will ever read your paper. Consequently take the time and effort to polish it into a small perfect shining crystal of succinct information.

PROPOSALS

Proposals for presenting at conferences are relatively easy to write. However writing proposals for grants is considerably more difficult. Both kinds are submitted electronically.

Proposals to Conferences

Writing proposals for presenting at conferences is similar to writing abstracts. Brevity is important but conferences seldom require the proposal to be as short as abstracts for journals. Each conference will have its proposal requirements and deadlines posted on its website. These must be followed carefully. Usually the conference prefers a one-page proposal that can appear in their program. If you are accepted, the conference may then notify you the date for submitting an expanded paper for publication in their proceedings. Submission of a paper for the proceedings is voluntary. The proceedings are usually published so that this gives you a publication. However, give careful consideration before having your work published this way because a science journal will not consider publishing work that has been published elsewhere.

Proposals for Grants

Writing a grant proposal is quite different from writing a proposal to present at a conference. Grant proposals are lengthy matters, requiring information about your research, the background for it, its purpose, and its value to the grant-giving organization. Each institution, each organization, and each federal government offering grants have different requirements for the writing of the grants which they will accept.

Most universities and industrial research laboratories have people skilled in grant writing who can help you. Also whoever is offering the grant will have detailed instructions for applying. Instructions will vary widely among grants. Many grant-offering organizations are willing to send you copies of old successful applications.

First-time applications for a grant are often unsuccessful, but do not be discouraged. If yours is rejected, detailed information about why it has been rejected will accompany the rejection. Next you should carefully rewrite the grant addressing the reasons it was rejected, and resubmit. Successful scientists who have received numerous grants tell us that they have often rewritten and resubmitted a grant

66

three times before it was finally accepted. Besides improving the grant each time, they learned more about writing successful grants in the best way possible: by experience.

LETTERS

> *This is the long and short of it.*
> *— Shakespeare*
> *Merry Wives of Windsor*
> *Act II, scene ii*

Cover Letters

Submissions to journals today are done electronically, and including a brief electronic cover letter is appropriate. Such letters are easy to write and have no need to be original, witty, or eloquent. [Figure 5.1 shows an example of a cover letter. Table 5.1 gives suggestions for closing words.]

Basically a cover letter simply tells the editors you have attached an article for their consideration and may include a brief list of other scientists in your field, who in your opinion would be appropriate for reviewing your work. The reason you supply names of 3–4 others in your field is to alert the editors about people who have expertise in the subject of your paper. The editors may or may not take your advice, but the help you give them may prevent them from sending your paper to inappropriate reviewers. Normally you do not include names of people at your university.

Editors
Journal of Important Science
1000 Hope Street
New York, NY, USA

February 20, 2006

Dear Editors,

Please consider the attached manuscript for publication in *The Journal of Important Science.*

Suitable reviewers for this manuscript, who are acquainted with this field of science, include:

- Prof. J. C. Maxwell, Chem. Dept., Institution, City, USA, email: mx@yahoo.edu.
- Prof. M. Genji, Materials Sci. Dept., Institution, City, Japan, email: gnj@matsci.jp.
- Dr. J. S. Bach, Research Dept., Company, City, Germany, email: jsbach@matris.de.

Sincerely,

– *Hong Mee*   *(Type your signature in italics, without a title)*

Dr. H. Mee, Associate Professor   *(Type your name, title,*
University   *address, telephone,*
City   *and email)*
Country
  tel: 609-731-4855, ext. 3
  email: nmee@university.edu

Figure 5.1   Example of a Cover Letter for Electronic Submission of an Article to a Science Journal

> *Men of few words are the best men.*
> *— Shakespeare*
> *King Henry V*
> *Act III, scene i*

Table 5.1   Suggestions for Closing Words for Use in Professional Letters.

Professional	Personal	Slightly Dated	Obsolete
• Sincerely,	• Warm	• Yours truly,	• Your humble
• Sincerely	regards,	• Respectfully	servant,
yours,	• All the best,	yours,	• With deep
• Yours,	• Best wishes,		respect,
• Yours	• Cheers,		• Humbly
sincerely,	• Best regards,		yours,

> *The better part of valour is discretion.*
> *— Shakespeare*
> *King Henry IV, Part I*
> *Act V, scene iv*

Introductory and Application Letters

Thabo Mbeki, speaking in South Africa, called the Internet more a social creation than a technological one (Crystal, 2001). Today most letters worldwide are sent and received over the Internet: letters to people we know and letters to those we are contacting for the first time. Corresponding through the Internet has changed the style of normal email correspondence enormously. We have become, some would say, frighteningly informal in the way many of us write to others. For many of us, this upsets a number of the letter-writing traditions we were taught.

Deciding what style to use when sending emails is your choice. However, choose your models carefully and consider what type of personality you desire to convey. Some kinds of language may be intended to be friendly but may actually appear to be so informal as to be impolite. For example, beginning an email message 'Hi,' or 'Hi Petey,' or 'Hi Dr. Young' when the recipient has not previously met nor communicated with the writer may shock the receiver.

Other greetings seem to be overly formal, 'My Very Dear Dr. Young' or 'Honored Professor'. There is nothing wrong with such greetings but they seem old-fashioned. At the other extreme, occasional emails arrive with no salutation beyond the name at the top and the subject line: This form of email seems rude when used to address someone who is not an old friend or who has not been involved in a continuing sequence of emails with you. The Internet permits us to respond more quickly and more efficiently than was even dreamed of in the days of postal mail; now the degree of what has been traditionally considered good manners is up to you.

Treat any email much as you would a letter by being sure to sign off with a word or phrase such as 'Sincerely', and on the line below, your name, without title. Probably at the bottom of each letter, your email automatically adds your

Date: Tue, 23 Feb 2006
From: K.J. Ping <kjing@hspt.ac.jo>
Subject: Application for a Postdoctoral Position
To: west@chem.wisc.edu

Dear Professor West,

I am a graduate student at Advanced Technical University in Berlin, Germany. I received my Ph.D., in October, 2005 and expect to complete studies for my Ph.D. degree by April or May 2007. My research has involved the study of the synthesis of optically active SiO-containing polymers and siloxane gels.

I am highly interested in the research in polymer being done in your laboratory, and would like to work in your group, if such a position is open. I would appreciate it very much if you would let me know about any such possibility.

I have attached a copy of my personal resume. My supervisor, Professor Dubono, will be happy to write a letter of recommendation for me, and other references are listed in my resume.

Yours sincerely,

– K. J. Ping

K.J. Ping
Department of Chemistry
Advanced Technical University
Berlin, Germany
kjing@hspt.ac.jo

Figure 5.2   Example of an Introductory Letter, Sent by Email

full name with title, your institution, telephone, and email. If you do not have this feature on your email, add the information at the left, a line or two below your typed signature. [Table 5.1]

The most effective letters of introduction or application are simple and direct. They are to the point, brief, and state only factual, relevant information. You attach your resume and perhaps one other relevant brief document, such as an abstract. Letters of recommendation are sent later by the people who are recommending you. Because letters of introduction or application are so brief, it is absolutely essential that you make no mistakes, even of a minor nature, in your English. Edit your letter, and have at least one other person edit it, before you send it. [Figure 5.2 gives an example of a letter of introduction and application.]

Keep a file of letters you send and letters you receive. These will serve you as a future resource for appropriate letter writing. The danger of email correspondence is that you may write so quickly that the English in it falls short of the level of excellence you want. The best advice is to compose your letters in a word-processing program, and then, after you are certain of their perfection, copy and paste them into email. The success this brings you will make the extra effort you give more than worthwhile.

> *A very good piece of work, I assure you, and a merry.*
> *— Shakespeare*
> *A Midsummer Night's Dream*
> *Act I, scene ii*

PART II

Presenting at International Conferences

Presenting good research at an international conference is everyone's desire, and many people's fear. However, if you are someone who has been ill-at-ease about presenting, you need be no longer, because the art of being a good presenter is something you can learn. The world of science needs to hear about the exciting and interesting work you do. Telling others about your research gives a gift to other scientists. Soon you will become involved in sharing internationally with many people. When you do this, science becomes friendlier, bigger, and better.

You have already written a successful abstract [See Chapter 5 on writing abstracts] and been accepted as a speaker. Congratulations. Now, at the conference you will be expected to speak, not read, your paper and to, talk about, not read, your slides.

Being successful as a presenter means being fully prepared. To become fully prepared you must not waste your energy by worrying. Some people spend a great deal of otherwise valuable time by worrying. Worrying is not helpful. Preparing is helpful. As a wise, fine scientist, you are going to be a successful presenter because you are going to be prepared.

Because Part I addresses writing and Part II addresses speaking, you will find significant differences in advice. For example, you learned in writing to: edit out all extraneous words; use transitions only when required; be careful in your use of polite but ambiguous verbs, such as could, would; and avoid the use of questions. Now you will find that in presenting, you may want deliberately to use some extraneous words in the forms of politeness, and language softeners in order to smooth the transition from slide to slide. You may find that asking questions with your voice or on a slide can now sometimes become an effective technique.

Fortunately for you, successful presenting is a much easier art to master than is the art of writing a paper for publication. These two arts walk hand in hand and help each other along the path to communicating science successfully.

- Chapter 6 helps you understand the role of slides.
- Chapter 7 gives techniques for making music with your voice.
- Chapter 8 deals with showing body bravery and practicing.
- Chapter 9 contains tongue-in-cheek advice on the art of napping.

– 6 –

The Art of Preparing Slides

As soon as you know you are going to speak, begin by preparing your slides. Choose titles, key words, graphics, citations, and think about color and design. Everything will become easier once you have prepared the slides. Unknown to you, all the time you are preparing slides, your mighty subconscious mind is preparing the ground for the words with which you will explain your slides. As you create your slides you are like a farmer planting seeds from which a garden will grow.

Today most scientists design and prepare their slides by using a software program, such as Microsoft's PowerPoint, to prepare either 1) a set of individual transparencies, which will be placed by hand on an overhead projector, or 2) a set of transparencies on a CD or a flash stick, which will be projected through a computer. Which way you choose to present is unimportant. Choose whichever way feels most comfortable to you. Each style has its advantages, and each is equally good. A wise presenter, however, carries a set of individual transparencies as a protection against electrical failure or unexpected computer incompatibility.

> *A Picture Is Worth a Thousand Words.*
> *– Chinese proverb*

BEING AN ARTIST

Computers permit us to make beautiful slides: They let us use color, insert photographs, and even add motion. However, please be gentle with your audience. Such additions such as color, photographs, or motion are good only if they help your slides be:

- clear
- legible
- easy-to-understand.

Unfortunately, software programs for creating slides have not, as we hoped, solved the problem of poor slides. However, such programs have made it much easier to create an excellent and memorable set of slides.

You are a scientist, and, when you make slides about your work, you also become an artist. Your aim is to create slides which add to, not distract from, your message. To make artistic slides you need to give as much thought to the size and placement of areas of space as you do to your use of print and color. In the end you want your slides to show that you care enough about your work to produce slides that are clear and pleasing to the eye but do not look like gaudy commercial advertisements. The audience appreciates a good set of slides but they are interested in your research not in how capable you are of using bizarre colors or images revolving or shooting in or out of the screen. Challenge your-self to make attractive but scientific looking slides.

> *We will draw the curtain and show you the picture.*
> *— Shakespeare*
> *The Tempest*
> *Act I, scene v*

Use of Color

International conferences yield both good and poor examples of the use of color. Next time you attend a conference note how color is used on the slides that are easiest for your eyes to understand. Make notes of ideas for your next set of slides, especially techniques that invite your slides to look like a set rather than a random assortment of slides.

Each computer program has background colors for slides. Pale colors, such as pale yellow, make a more interesting background than a plain screen, but choose a background color that does not interfere with the clarity of the information on the slide. Notice that a bright-colored background makes seeing the information on the slide difficult. Backgrounds come in the form of 1) templates that can be used on all or selected slides, and 2) 'fill' colors by which you can vary the background or effectively leave the screen white in areas behind print. Further any of the colors can be toned brighter or paler.

Many of the programs for specific sciences, such as ChemDraw, have a limited and rather glaring choice of color, but the main program has a wide and tasteful assortment. So when using programs for symbols specific to your science, switch back into the main program, in order to apply color that pleases the eye and doesn't clash. Highlighting words in primary colors of bright red and bright blue, for example, is less pleasing than using the same colors but in a red with some orange or pink in it, and a blue with some green or red in it. The palette of colors available is excellent; take some time to find good colors.

Too many colors, say a total of 5 and up, on one slide is usually not only less pleasant but less effective than 2–4. However at a recent international conference one highly effective slide used 9–10 colors between the fill colors and the print colors. So, do it your way, but be kind to the eyes of your audience. Purple and red, for example, are usually not pleasing on the same slide, especially when the shade of red is towards the orange.

Background fill color can help clarify information when it is necessary to have a list that fills the slide. A band of a single pale fill color behind one item on the list alternates with a band of the screen color behind the next item. This is effective when a great deal of information must be listed on one slide and only a total of two colors are used behind the print.

CHOOSING FONT STYLES AND SIZE OF PRINT

Fonts

On slides the simpler fonts, such as 'Arial', are easier to read on a screen than more traditional fonts with serifs, such as 'Times New Roman'. Generally using bold throughout is easiest to read, especially if you have both a large screen and a large audience. At any rate avoid using a variety of serif and non-serif fonts on the same slide in order to avoid distracting the eyes of the audience in ways that hinder their reading and understanding of the slide. Lower-case letters are easier to read than all capitals.

Print Size

Keep the size of print for words and numbers as large as possible. In most programs anything smaller than point-18 cannot be read on the screen by all the audience. This may mean you need to make a larger number of slides and put less information on each slide. You want the people at the back of the room to be able to read all the information, including the citations. To do this you must 1) limit the number of words on each slide, and 2) discipline yourself to put as little information on each slide as possible, using your voice to fill in the information.

An audience at a conference becomes annoyed with a speaker when there is so much information on a slide that they cannot follow the speaker's logic. Unfortunately this becomes particularly true when the audience also has trouble understanding the speaker's English.

ADDING EMPHASIS

Add emphasis to your slide through the use of color and by putting the most important information in a larger print size, down to the least important in smaller size.

Take care that even your smallest print can be read by the audience, making use of abbreviations where necessary. Then make your choices consistent throughout the set of slides.

Italics are sometimes used effectively to add emphasis. However underlining is not effective. A form of emphasis that is seldom considered to be in good taste is the use of exclamation points. A total of one exclamation point might occur on an entire set of slides without appearing to add an unprofessional touch to the presentation.

You will decrease your need for emphasis if you avoid putting whole sentences or lengthy phrases on your slides and instead using only key words or brief phrases. This permits you to give effective emphasis by what words you choose, your tone of voice, where you pause, and the words you stress. The audience will appreciate your style and understand your slides better.

NUMBERING ITEMS

Be cautious about numbering items on your slides that do not require numbers. If you are only indicating a list of points or details avoid labeling with numerals: 1, 2, 3 . . .; I, II, III . . .; i, ii, iii . . . or implied numerals: a, b, c . . . Numbering is should be used only when you are emphasizing chronology or priority. Otherwise numbering is embarrassingly meaningless and should be replaced with bullets, dashes, or some other appropriate symbol.

DETERMINING THE NUMBER OF SLIDES

Here are the steps for determining how many slides you need:

- First, assemble the slides you have.
- Second, arrange them into a good sequence.
- Third, practice explaining them.
- Fourth, time yourself as you explain each: Ideally each slide is explained in a slow careful voice in a minute (or much less).
- Fifth, add, subtract, or combine slides so that each can be explained in a minute or less AND the total come within your allotted time.

CHOOSING TITLES AND WORDS

Titles are important. A title states the topic of the slide as simply and as briefly as possible. Titles should look like titles: Perhaps yours will be enclosed in colored boxes, written in larger print or in all caps. At any rate, in some way your titles must signal clearly that they are titles and that the information they contain is vital to understanding the slide. Titles are clearer and more emphatic if they are written as topics, not as complete sentences.

Rarely if ever do good slides contain complete sentences anywhere, even in conclusions. Complete sentences on a slide put a presenter in an embarrassing position, because the speaker is then forced to read aloud to an audience. Reading sentences aloud to a literate audience is insulting to them. A literate audience has already seen the words and read them for themselves before you have finished saying them. Your voice then sounds repetitious and uninteresting, and the attention of the audience wanders at the very time you most wanted them to pay attention. So what is the solution? The solution is to use key words and phrases on the slides and let your voice complete the information, adding interest and details. Otherwise, especially in the conclusion, you will end on a slightly boring note. No one wants to complete a presentation on a boring note.

COMPLETING YOUR SET OF SLIDES

The Credit Slide

An important slide is the one in which you give credit to those who have worked with you or financed your research. If there is time, read these names aloud to give honor. Usually the slide contains only their names and your voice adds titles or other information, such as the institution and country. Often this slide is last, but it can also be first. Placement is unimportant. What is important is that the credit slide is there somewhere so that others always receive appropriate credit.

The Final Result

You want to make every effort to complete your slides so that the final result looks like a set. Perhaps you are using several slides you have used in the past. Fine, but now redo them so that they match the others in this presentation.

Chapter 6

Fortunately the ability to scan in material and the help of computer software make it easy to redo old slides so that they become a professional-looking part of a set. So, take the time to make your slides have some common elements that help them look like a set. Ideally throughout the set you have already used the same style of font, varieties of color, and emphasis techniques on each slide. Perhaps you have chosen to use the same background fill of pale color throughout, or you may have invented some other distinctive but still tasteful touch to make it clear that your slides are a set.

The best result will be a set of slides that serves information kaiseki style. 'Kaiseki' is a quietly impressive way of serving food at elegant banquets in Japan. Many, small, attractive, well-prepared dishes, are served sequentially and with grace. Think of your presentation as a banquet and your slides as the food.

Then serve your information by putting only a small, tasty dish on each slide. Ideally you will have many slides, each requiring less than a minute of explanation. This way the information on your slides will be clear, and the minds of the audience can feast happily on your well-prepared information.

Now, you have a complete and tasteful set of slides, and now all you have to do is to become master of your slides. You will show the audience you are the master, not the victim, of your slides by the music of your voice and by your body language.

Why, then the world's mine oyster.
— Shakespeare
Merry Wives of Windsor
Act II, scene ii

– 7 –

The Art of Using Your Voice

The tune of English may be different than the music of the language in which you usually speak. If so you may have to learn to sing a new melody – a melody in which stress is vitally important. English is a stress-timed language more than a syllable-timed language. So, although pronunciation is important, it will have less effect on whether or not your English is understood than using the correct stress will.

> *Friends, Romans, countrymen, lend me your ears;*
> *– Shakespeare*
> *Julius Caesar*
> *Act III, scene ii*

STRESS AND ACCENT

Linguists and dictionaries have not yet agreed upon exact pronunciations in either standard British English or standard American English, but they usually agree on placement of stress. So match your use of stress to that of some native speaker of English and you have relatively little to worry about.

85

If you have the stress right, you should not waste your time by worrying about whether or not you have some kind of accent. Everyone has an accent. Even a person born and raised within an English-speaking country has some form of regional accent.

Perhaps as English simplifies and becomes even more international, a universally accepted set of pronunciations will develop, but that hasn't happened yet. And don't hold your breath waiting for it.

PITCH

So whatever English accent you use, treat your voice like the magnificent musical instrument it is. First, learn how to pitch your voice so that you will not strain it when you speak to an audience. Control the pitch of your voice by projecting the sound, not from the upper throat or nasal passages but from the diaphragm and lower throat. This type of deep projection makes your voice more pleasant to listen to. It keeps the 'roundness' of the sound of your voice and maintains warmth. In contrast, when you pitch your voice high, you strain your voice box: Your throat easily tires, and your voice sounds 'thin'.

VOLUME

We speak to friends and family with less volume than is needed when speaking to an audience. Successful speakers must increase the volume as well as the depth of their normal speaking voice. In fact you need to increase the volume and depth of your voice even when using electronic amplification because otherwise your voice will not sound as full and warm as it can.

Chapter 7

Gender Differences

Male and female voice differences are as socially induced as they are physically caused. Of course, there is a difference between male and female vocal cords. However this would not be such a strong difference had we not been encouraged by our cultures to deliberately pitch our voices high for women and low for men.

Women who let their voices go high in their throats instead of deeper into their chests sound a bit like children. Maybe this is intentional; maybe not. However, childlike tones of stress and pitch may invite listeners to assume speakers are less professional than they are. All of us, male or female, can train ourselves to speak in deeper, fuller tones.

Both male and female voices are sometimes soft and difficult to hear. With friends or in a small group a soft voice may be considered polite. However in a larger group soft, quiet speech signals that the speaker is uncertain, and that perhaps the audience should question the factuality of what is being said. All of us can train ourselves to increase the volume of our voices.

> *I talk to you: Why did you wish me milder? Would you have me false to my nature? Rather say I play the man I am.*
>
> *– Shakespeare*
> *Coriolanus*
> *Act III, scene ii*

SPEED

Once you have practiced increasing the loudness of your voice, you will want to concentrate on speaking slower and with more animation than you normally speak. Get someone, preferably who speaks good English, to help you decide which words or phrases you choose to emphasize in order to make an interesting English-sounding melody.

Research by mathematicians and linguists tell us that human languages around the world are spoken at about the same speed. Individuals within each language speak at varied rates, and this variation is about the same in all languages. Yet, most people believe other languages are spoken more rapidly than theirs. An unfortunate consequence of this is that when you speak a language, such as English, in which you feel less comfortable than in your native tongue, you may speed up. You probably are doing this under the false assumption that English is spoken more rapidly than it actually is.

Success speaking at a conference requires speech that is slower and clearer than occurs in normal conversation. However, nervousness can also invite one to speak too rapidly. If this is true of you, you may have a double problem achieving a loud, slow speed, but with practice and careful timing you can do it. (See Chapter 7 for advice on practicing and timing.)

READING TO AN AUDIENCE

The most important thing to remember is that the audience and speaker together form a speech. Avoid reading sentences on slides to the audience. Your audience is highly literate and beyond doubt they can read English faster and better than they can hear it. So try not to insult them by reading to them exactly what is already there for them to see. The solution of course is to use key words or phrases rather than sentences on your slides. This way you can glance at the slide and then put key words into full sentences as you explain the slide, adding meaning to what they read. This will invite the audience to feel honored and will prevent you from feeling foolish for saying what they can clearly read.

Don't Read Your Paper Aloud

The only good advice about reading a paper aloud to an audience is 'Don't'. It is boring and ineffective. Possibly at some time in your career you will find it necessary to read a paper to an audience because the person scheduled to present is absent. However never let this happen when you have time to prepare. If against your best wishes you are ever forced to read a paper, the solution is to know the material so thoroughly that you are able to look frequently at the audience, project your voice enthusiastically, and only occasionally glance down at the print.

Sadly enough even though they know better, occasional presenters still read instead of speak their papers. Perhaps they believe their English will sound better when they read, but this is never true. Listening to someone read a paper is always difficult for an audience. When someone reads science aloud the voice tends to become sing-song and monotonous, whereas the information becomes alive and interesting when an audience can see a speaker talk, look, smile, and gesture. So do whatever you can to make your information new and exciting. Permit yourself to have a communication with the audience that goes beyond words.

Speakers' success suffers when they read papers aloud because they are forced to bend their heads to look at the paper. This not only prevents the audience from seeing their facial expression but it constricts their throats so that their voices are harder to understand. The final sadness is that when speakers read to an audience, they usually hide behind a podium or table. Standing behind a table or podium is always a disadvantage because it signals that the speaker wants distance from the audience.

However, if, for one reason or another, you cannot avoid reading a paper aloud, you can somewhat compensate by looking up at the audience as frequently as possible and keeping at least one of your hands free to establish non-verbal communication (see Chapter 8). You can consider preparing your paper by:

- Putting accent marks on syllables to be stressed.
- Marking places where your voice should pause.
- Underlining phrases to emphasize.
- And, above all, practicing aloud (see Chapter 8).

SOFT WORDS

Your slides are ready. Your voice is ready. Now what words will you choose? Your spreadsheets and the articles you photocopied will supply you with good choices of verbs, adjectives, and phrases, but they will not supply you with soft words to smooth the audience's way between slides. They are not in the articles you photocopied for these are words used verbally. In final drafts of published research articles, they are edited out as extraneous language.

But now you need them. You need the very words and phrases you edit out when you write. You need them in your voice, not on your slides. You want some simple words to serve as 'softeners'/'smoothers' as you lead the audience from one slide to the next. Find these words by listening for them at conferences when you hear English speakers present. Figure 1 contains a list of some heard recently at an international conference.

Listen for soft transitions when you hear English speakers at conferences. Choose the ones you like and make a list to add to your spreadsheets.

You might also consider a transitional word or phrase from your language or another language. Anything is superior to 'um uh . . .', 'er ah . . .', 'ummm . . .'. For example,

. . . as you see . . .
. . . having said this . . .
. . . once again we . . .
. . . and, yes, the . . .
. . . well . . .
. . . for example . . .
. . . now to our surprise . . .
. . . actually . . .
. . . anyhow . . .
. . . all right, so . . .

Figure 7.1   Transition Words Used as Softeners

you might choose something with a meaning similar to the English words: 'OK . . .', 'and . . .', 'so . . .', 'yes . . .', 'furthermore . . .', or 'next . . .'. Such a word or phrase in your native language could – with profit and no loss of audience understanding – add an ethnic international touch which might delight an audience and add to the pleasure of hearing your presentation.

> *Be not afraid of greatness; some are born great, some achieve greatness . . .*
>
> *– Shakespeare*
> *Twelfth Night*
> *Act II, scene v*

– 8 –

The Art of Body Language and Presenting Smoothly

What an amazing amount of courage it takes for any of us to stand before an audience. Every speaker, no matter how famous, needs bravery to speak to an audience. Your bravery is increased because you are able to communicate in two languages: The language of speech and the language of the body.

> *Our doubts are traitors, and make us lose the good we oft might win, by fearing to attempt.*
> *– Shakespeare*
> *Measure for Measure*
> *Act I, scene iv*

Your stance, how you move, and your facial and hand gestures tell the audience about you. According to Arnold and Roach (1989), non-verbal messages often take precedence over verbal and communicate more. Psychologists tell us the words we use comprise at best only 30% of communication.

This is good news to those of us whose English is poor, to those of us who dislike speaking, and to those of us who have slides. Now, how to use your body to communicate the messages you want to give the audience? You need good eye contact as well as a stance and gestures that show your courage.

EYE CONTACT

Whether you are brave or not, you must appear brave. The easiest way to appear brave – the magic touch of a good presenter – is to look directly at the audience. This gives the impression of being confident about your material. In your personal life you look at people when you talk to them. The secret for success with an audience is to appear to be having a conversation with them.

Look at them. Look at those to the left, to the right, in the front, in the back. Watch them intently to show how much you want them to understand. They will listen more intently and understand much better when they realize how much you want them to understand.

Look steadily at them. First at those in one place and then at those in another, looking at each place for 5–10 seconds or longer. If it distracts you to look directly into faces, look at the level of their faces but between faces. No one in a large audience will be able to tell you are not looking directly into someone's eyes. (Don't try this at parties or during coffee breaks or you will be thought of as evasive or extremely absentminded.) Beware of looking at the floor, or at the ceiling as you speak: The audience knows no one is lying down there, or hanging up there, and will wonder why you appear to be trying to make eye contact the table or the chandelier.

Above all, do not let yourself be taken hostage by 'PowerPoint' and the screen. Technology has permitted you to make beautiful slides; now trust it to remain in place behind you or beside you. Glancing only briefly at the screen to remind yourself what the audience is seeing or to use the laser occasionally to emphasize a point. Generally keep your eyes on the audience and earn their respect.

KEEPING AN 'OPEN BODY'

Keeping your body open to the audience means keeping the entire front of your body facing the audience as fully, and as much, as possible. An expert will avoid hiding behind a podium or table. Step out. Step close to the audience and make them your friends.

Covering the front of your body with your arm/s suggests you wish to hide the essence of who you are. Try to keep your arms and gestures open to the audience. Above all, avoid turning your back and speaking at the same time. English has an idiom about 'turning one's back on something', which means rejecting it. So make all gestures at the screen with the arm closest to the screen so that you do not cross your body with your arm or turn your back. Instead trust the screen, know your slides, and give your attention to the audience not the screen. A brief glance will be enough to remind you what each slide contains, and then you – like the expert you are – can look at the audience as you speak.

Moving some as you present is fine. For example, you look good when you walk a bit as you speak or gesture. However, you want to avoid rocking back and forth, which distracts the audience, and particularly avoid stepping backwards. Moving backwards signals you are unsure; you want to keep the audience from thinking you are unsure about what you are presenting.

Some presenters worry about what to do with their hands. The best thing to do with your hands is not to think about them. Think about science. Then use your hands to get your message across and to show your enthusiasm. The audience deserves to see that you enjoy what you do.

Work on developing some easy open-hand gestures with your other hand that will help you explain your work. What is natural for you to do with your hands when you have a friendly talk with friends or family? Observe yourself from within, and then use these gestures to help you when you want to communicate with an audience. Particularly effective gestures are any in which your palms are up, fingers spread, or the thumb and another finger touch each other.

Audiences appreciate speakers who show they have opened their minds by speaking with their hands and arms as well as with their slides and voices. You will look informed, confident, and experienced.

USING A LASER

One of your hands may be holding a laser, which can so drive an audience crazy that possibly scientists should not be permitted to handle this terrible instrument. However, the laser has one great advantage: It gives one of your hands something to do. If you use it, use it correctly.

The Off Button

The most important part of a laser is the Off button. Even some world-famous scientists have shown they do not understand the use of the Off button. Instead they have used a dancing, jumping light as they talk. The light flashes up/down–left/right–zig/zag–circle/swirl: The audience can hardly hear or see the good science because their eyes try to follow the path of light as it sweeps irrationally around the screen. The speaker knows what the light is trying to emphasize, but the audience does not. Consequently, the audience's comprehension and concentration fade. Your job as a presenter is to learn to use the laser correctly, or not to use it at all.

When you use a laser, employ a single, steady spot of light to show the audience where to look. Use a 2–3 second spot of light, indicating the exact location of the information you are about to explain. Keep the light steady; your voice silent; then snap the laser off and talk. A moving streak of light confuses the audience about where they should look and when you talk at the same time you flash the laser, the light will flicker about and distract the audience from hearing your words. Watch at your next conference and notice how a light flying about the screen like a nervous butterfly makes reading diagrams extraordinarily difficult. Your audience consists of intelligent people who want to study and understand your slides. Let them.

Once you have learned to master the Off button you show the audience: 1) You are a skilled presenter, 2) You know your slides well, and 3) You respect your listeners.

Which Hand and How to Stand

Where you stand and in which hand you hold the laser is an important part of your body language. When you stand to the left of the screen, use the laser in your right hand; when you stand to the right of the screen, use the laser in your left hand. If you move as you talk so that you go to the other side of the screen, switch the hand holding the laser so that you do not either put your arm across your body or turn your back to the audience. Be brave. Face them all the time and do it without closing your body off with your arms.

Recently in Philadelphia, a presenter giving a plenary lecture at an international meeting displayed an unusual and effective technique. He steadied his laser hand by putting his other hand on the wrist of the hand holding the laser. This way he could hold the spot steady for several seconds. He did not turn his back nor look at the screen himself for more than a brief glance. He was well-prepared: He knew what was on his slides; he showed the audience he knew. He was an expert. You can be one too.

PRACTISING

Once you have become comfortable with your slides, your voice, and your body, you will have accomplished the basics. Most importantly, you will have timed your speech so that you never have the embarrassment of going over your allotted time.

All presenting techniques must be practiced and most scientists would rather do science than practice speaking. However, developing the type of speech-giving persona which suits you only has to be done once. Then it is yours forever, and you can get back to what is important: discovering new ideas in science. So give your speech-giving self the practice it needs, and you can be a speech-making success for the rest of your life.

> *This above all: to thine own self be true.*
> *— Shakespeare*
> *Hamlet*
> *Act I, scene iii*

Preparation

Your slides are ready. You have chosen what to say. Now you must practice aloud going through your slides, always timing yourself. You may find you have no choice but to leave out some important material, so save those slides for some other use. Practicing aloud is the only way you can be sure you will stay within the allotted time. You never want to have the experience of having your audience grow restless and annoyed, or forcing the chair of the session to tell you to stop.

Once you have learned to control the volume and depth of your voice, speaking to a large audience is usually easier than speaking to an audience of 8–15 because the anonymous character of a large audience helps you to lose embarrassment.

Two warnings

Experts advise us to avoid practicing by looking into a mirror – the person in the mirror distracts us and does not make a helpful audience. We are also warned that although practicing in front of a small group of other professionals or students is helpful, surprisingly enough practicing in front of one's family is extremely difficult and often not helpful.

Your Conference Persona

Now you are ready to practice your whole conference persona. One way to do this is to imagine that three walls of an empty room represent your audience and the fourth wall the screen behind you. Imagine the three walls are rows of interested scientists. Now tell them your story by explaining your slides to them. Glance only briefly at your slides on the screen behind you. Keep your body, as much as possible, turned toward the audience. Maintain eye contact with your imaginary audience, talk, move, and gesture. Invite yourself to feel comfortable as you tell your story. Last, remember to check your time. You are now forming habits for a lifetime of success as a speaker.

Practice your speech as if you are having a conversation with a friend. Use every technique you can think of to avoid a monotone or a repetitious, rocking rhythm. An audience enjoys hearing warmth in your voice. It is a sign you enjoy science. The audience wants you to like what you do; you want the audience to like what they hear: A perfect fit for success. Your secret is to be loud, clear, enthusiastic, and slow, slow . . . slow – explaining your work as carefully and with as much excitement as you would like other scientists to use when they explain their work to you.

> *Wisely and slow; they stumble that run fast.*
> *– Shakespeare*
> *Romeo and Juliet*
> *Act II, scene iii*

ENDING ON TIME

Lewis Carroll (1866) in *Through the Looking Glass* warned '. . . Beware the Jabberwocky . . .' The lack of good timing of your presentation could be your Jabberwocky. Beware.

You will be given a certain number of minutes in which to speak. Typically this is 20 minutes, which includes time for someone to introduce you and time at the end for you to answer questions. Be prepared to accept that whatever length of time you are given it will not be enough to explain your research in full detail. However, it is vital that you stay within your time limit. Vital.

Nothing angers the audience or the organizers more than a speaker who goes overtime. Either the next speaker will have less time or the schedule of the whole conference will be delayed – and you, you, will be the Jabberwocky who caused it.

Here is the way to stay within an allotted number of minutes: First you must force yourself to be realistic about how much you can explain, slowly and carefully, in the length of time you are given. Perhaps you have valuable, lengthy results, which need explanation of procedure, background, and future possibilities. Too bad, too bad, but that is how it is: You are given a limited number of minutes. You cannot tell them everything. You will 1) choose what is most important, 2) display it in clear, uncluttered slides, and 3) explain each slide in slow, simple, easy-to-understand English. Racing through a bewildering amount of rapid data is the worst mistake a presenter can make.

YOUR FINAL WORDS

At the end of your speech simply say 'Thank you.' This is the best and kindest way to let the audience know that you have finished. Do not worry about ending a bit early. No one has ever been upset when speakers end early but they are easily upset by those who speak too long. Should you end early, there is no embarrassment: You will have more time for comments and the next speaker will appreciate your courtesy.

FIELDING QUESTIONS

Usually after your talk, there is time for questions and comments from the audience. Ideally during the question period, the chair will repeat questions or comments so that they are clear. But this is not always an ideal world, so if this doesn't happen, you ask the questioner to repeat the question so that the whole audience can hear it – and so you can hear it again and have additional time to think. Keep your voice up at this time, listen intently, and step toward the questioner. Don't back away. Take your time. You are the speaker; you are in control here, not the questioner.

You do not need to fear this question period because, for some psychological reason, by the end of a presentation, the audience is instinctively on your side. They have come to identify so thoroughly with you and your science that they will come to your aid to protect you from strange or difficult questions. So depend on the audience and be ready to ask:

- if someone in the audience will help you answer,
- the questioner to rephrase the question,
- the questioner to come talk to you after the session,

or be ready to say:

- 'I do not understand your question, please explain,
- 'That is a good question; I will think about it,
- 'I wish I could answer that.

Remember this period of questions and comments may be valuable to you. By listening intently to what people in the audience say, you may get important insights for your future research.

Stand straight, smile, and look confident, for you have now developed the persona of a fine presenter. You have taught yourself to keep your mind on your desire to 1) tell your story, 2) communicate ideas, and 3) make science a little bit bigger and better. You have learned to forget about yourself and concentrate on communicating with the audience. You are an accomplished and professional presenter.

> *Your own resolution to succeed is more important than any other one thing*
> *— Library cornerstone, Waynesburg College, Waynesburg, Pennsylvania, USA*

– 9 –

The Art of Napping at Conferences

How to nap at conferences and seminars without damaging one's reputation as a serious scientist is an important consideration for participants at conferences. Chapter 9 deals only with the 30-second to three-minute nap. Napping activities over this time limit, especially those that fall into deep sleep, are beyond the scope of this chapter.

During conferences, particularly international conferences, frequent short naps, interspersed with periods of wakefulness during a single conference session, appear not only likely to occur but possibly should be encouraged as a form of brain preservation.

The safest environment for a successful nap is within the setting of a large conference. Napping within groups of ten or less is a supreme challenge even to an inveterate napper and you should avoid napping in small groups until you have thoroughly studied this chapter.

First, before discussing techniques, a word about nodding: Nodding is that all-revealing jerky movement of the head as you alternately relax muscular tension as you slip into sleep and then recover. This activity should be avoided: It is likely to cause a neckache and, worst of all, it will enable everyone to see that you are indeed napping. Using one or more of the techniques developed here, skilled conference attendees are generally able to avoid this revealing nodding or bobbing of the head and thus preserve the pretence of being awake and listening even when the eyes are closed.

Selection of a proper napping technique generally depends on from whom you are trying to conceal your activity: the speaker, people sitting beside you, or people sitting behind you. The latter, naturally, is the easiest to accomplish and usually requires only adequate head support to prevent nodding. A situation in which the conference members are seated in the round or in a horseshoe arrangement poses special problems and requires the full resourcefulness of the napper.

> *I am a man more sinned against than sinning.*
> *– Shakespeare*
> *King Lear*
> *Act III, scene ii*

Variations of successful napping techniques developed over the years include:

- The **DG**. The most time-honored napping technique, is the **DG** (dark glasses) technique. In this technique care should be taken to select the darkest lenses when preparing for a conference. In addition, the glasses should be worn at the gathering prior to the talks so that the other conference goers will assume dark glasses are needed for your vision and not just a camouflage for napping. (One can oftentimes get insight into the reputation of the speaker by counting the number in the audience who are wearing dark glasses.)

- The **SE**. The **SE** (slit eyes) technique has been used successfully over the years but requires a degree of sophistication. Here, the eyes are not fully closed – a view of at least a miniscule portion of the white of the eyes must be preserved for this method to be successful. Eyelid fluttering must be carefully controlled and a general demeanor of fixed concentration should be maintained. Head support is optional.

- The **HOE**. The **HOE** (hands over eyes) technique is widely used and requires only a modicum of practice. A number of variations of the **HOE** are available:

  - The **HOF**. In the **HOF** (hands on forehead) variation, the eyes are concealed to simulate reading. If possible a spread-fingers position should be utilized since the closed-fingers position is, although it has certain advantages, a bit blatant. If you also choose to use decoy reading material, care should be taken to position it so that such material does not fall to the floor during the actual napping period, thus revealing your true activity.

  - The **HIH**. The **HIH** (hands in hair) variation is done with the head deeply bent, thus effectively putting the eyes on a horizontal plane where they are not observable except in the unlikely instance of people getting down on their knees to peer up into your face. (Note that this variation can become dangerous if employed after the halfway point of a session because this mode is highly conducive to complete sleep.) Care should be taken that your head does not slip off its hand support since, once the head goes all the way down to the table, napping becomes public knowledge. Many people successfully use this variation by keeping a copy of the program conspicuously open in front of them.

- The **FOE**. The **FOE** (fingers on eyes) is a variation of the **HOE** activity in which it is permissible to close the eyes completely and keep them closed for the period of the nap. It is a convincing ploy, if you wear glasses, to put the fingers up under the glasses and hold the eyes shut. This has the added advantage of giving some head support. However extreme care must be taken not to nod or fall into a deep sleep and knock the glasses off.

> *He does it with a better grace, but I do it more natural.*
>
> *– Shakespeare*
> *Twelfth Night*
> *Act II, scene iii*

- **One & One**. The **One & One** is a recently developed technique, which unfortunately requires a great deal of practice. In this method the eye on the observed side (the side next to the people you most want to convince that you are awake) is kept open while the other eye is closed to obtain the maximum benefit from the nap. Some users

108

report difficulty with this technique because it requires a good deal of coordination.

Just this month a field report mentions a new variation on the **One & One** in which the head is rested on the fist, which is supported by an elbow on the table. The cheek is then distended in such a way as to close the eye forcibly. The other eye remains open.

An added benefit of this variation is that it gives the impression of extreme boredom. Consequently this offers great potential for recently initiated conference goers who desire to display a degree of sophistication in their napping technique. Not nearly as much muscular control is required as in the straight **One & One**. (Please note that if a napper closes the unfisted eye, the activity will no longer qualify as a **One & One**)

- The **DFM**. The **DFM** (diversionary finger movement) is a technique suggested only for veteran nappers who have a great deal of coordination. In this skillful activity, both eyes may remain closed but the fingers remain in motion. Props, such as pencils or pens, may be used but most common is for just the fingers to maintain a drumming movement on the forehead. Deep sleep represents a particular danger in this technique, and novices are warned against attempting it until they have many hours of successful conference napping to their credit.

- The **HTB**. The **HTB** (head thrown back) may be a useful technique if the speaker is either exceptionally boring or exceptionally profound. In this technique, the head is thrown full back as if the napper is contemplating the ceiling. The difficulty here is that a great deal of finesse must be exercised in maintaining one's balance. In fact this position is not recommended unless the conference chairs have suitably high backs due to the severe injuries which can be sustained in the unfortunate circumstance that you fall backwards out of your chair.

> *Tempt not a desperate man*
>
> *– Shakespeare*
> *Romeo and Juliet*
> *Act V, scene iii*

As in all professional activities, in the art of successful napping certain things are to be strenuously avoided. Foremost among these is snoring. Snoring is widely considered to be a sign of deep sleep, and deep sleep automatically disqualifies a person from being considered a napper – although recently there has been some dissent on this view.

Please realize that other actions can betray you even after you have completed a successful nap. The worst is yawning. Yawning is unforgivable. Furthermore, looking around slyly after a successful nap to see if anyone has been watching is definitely bad form. Nodding is, of course, to be avoided. However, it is not as disastrous as losing muscular control so that the head rests upon the table or one falls out of the chair. (If the latter circumstance should ever occur it is considered best to pick yourself up and walk quickly from the hall.)

Veteran nappers will find they can be especially blatant about their napping by disarming observers with a well-timed, meaningless question after the speaker finishes. Developing a personal repertoire of suitable questions is important but some universally used questions which you can pattern after include:

- 'In the long run, what, in your opinion, is the significance of the conclusions you have drawn on the field as a whole?'
  (If you decide to use this question, you must be the first questioner after the speaker has finished; otherwise some non-napper will have used it.)

- 'What exactly do you mean by . . .?'
  (Choose a word from the title or first sentence of the speech before you begin to nap.)

- 'How do you reconcile what you have told us with the research done by . . .?'
  (Here either give the name of the most famous scientist in the field or use a name no one knows.)

Good luck in your attendance at international conferences, and if, despite all the advice in this chapter on successful napping, you choose to remain awake throughout the talks, a highly satisfying activity besides listening is available to you. You can entertain yourself by watching the other nappers. If you then discover additional techniques for successful napping, please contact the author of this book so they can be considered for the next edition.

> *We are such stuff*
>   *As dreams are made on . . .*
>   *— Shakespeare*
>   *The Tempest*
>   *Act IV, scene i*

Sources

Arnold, V.D. & Roach, T.D. (1989) "Teaching: A Non-Verbal Communication Event". *Business Education Forum*. October.

Asimov, Issac (1970) *Asimov's Guide to Shakespeare*. Avenel Books, New York, NY.

Axell, Roger E. (1995) *Do's & Taboos of Using English Around the World*. John Wiley & Sons, Inc. New York, NY.

Barzun, J. (1975). *Simple & Direct: A Rhetoric for Writers*. Harper & Row: New York, NY.

Bauer, L. & Trudgill, P. (1998) *Language Myths*. Penguin Books: London.

Blake, G. & Bly, R. (1993). *The Elements of Technical Writing*. Macmillan: New York, NY.

Cameron, J. (1999). *The Right to Write: An Invitation and Initiation into the Writing Life*. Penguin Putnam: New York, NY.

Crystal, D. (1997) *The Cambridge Encyclopedia of Language*, 2nd ed. Cambridge University Press: Cambridge, MA.

Crystal, D. (1998) *Language Play*. The University of Chicago Press: Chicago.

Crystal, D. (2001). *Language and the Internet*. Cambridge University Press: Cambridge, MA.

Crystal, D. (2003) *English as a Global Language*, 2nd ed. Cambridge University Press: Cambridge, MA.

Ebel, H.F., Bliefert, C., Russey, W.E. (2004) *The Art of Scientific Writing*. Wiley: New York.

113

Eisenberg, A. (2001). Spontaneous, Unedited, Naked: A Linguist Looks at Discourse on the Internet, *Scientific American*, December, 96–7

Garmston, R.J. & Wellman, B.M. (1992) *How to Make Presentations that Teach and Transform*. Association for Supervision and Curriculum Development: Alexandria, VA.

Hairston, M. & Ruszkiewicz, J.J. (1996). *The Scott, Foresman Handbook for Writers,* 4th ed. Harper Collins College Publishers: New York, NY.

Latour, B. (1987) *Science in Action*, Harvard University Press: Cambridge, MA.

MacNeil, R. (1989). *Wordstruck*. Penguin Books: New York, NY.

Microsoft Encarta College Dictionary (2001). St Martin's Press: NY.

Montgomery, S.L. (2003) *The Chicago Guide to Communicating Science*. University of Chicago Press: Chicago, IL.

Negrino, T. (2005) *Creating a Presentation in PowerPoint*, Peachpit Press: Berkeley, CA.

Random House Webster's College Dictionary, 2nd ed. (1999). Random House: New York, NY.

Schoenfeld, R. (1986) *The Chemist's English,* 2nd ed. VCH Verlagsgesellschaft: Federal Republic of Germany.

Shakespeare, W. Complete works placed on line in public domain 1993: www-tech.mit.edu/shakespeare/works.html

Shertzer, M.D. (1986). *The Elements of Grammar*. Macmillan: New York, NY.

Strunk, Jr. W., & White, E.B. (1979). *The Elements of Style*. Allyn Bacon: Needham, MS.

Afterword

The world's 6 billion people today live in a total of some 200 countries, speak over 6000 languages, and use some 2,260 writing systems. Amazing that out of this plethora of riches, English seemingly offers the only current possibility for worldwide communication.

Perhaps when linguists resolve the intriguing but intricate relationship between language and thought, we may know the extent to which the use of English enhances, changes, or inhibits scientific thinking. At present we have little idea of what we gain and what we lose when we commit to communicating science in English. But the time for philosophic thought about the effect of becoming increasingly dependent on English for international communication has passed.

Like it or not, English has become the Rosetta Stone of science. Consequently if we are all to understand each other accurately, scientific English must become more direct and clearer than it is at present. This means not only do you have to try harder, but all native speakers when writing or speaking to an international community of scientists, must be willing to give up their colorful, regional, and often mysterious use of idiomatic English. The evolution of international, scientific English will be up to all of us, and in it may lie new, shared scientific discoveries for the benefit of the planet we love.

However, may we not become so engrossed in exchanging valuable scientific information accurately that we lose the patterns of thought, the excitement, the beauty in the stories, drama, poetry of all languages. These provide the nourishment that keeps good science alive, and, without them, science loses its vision.

> *Here, I hope, begins our lasting joy.*
> *— Shakespeare*
> *Henry VI, Part III*
> *Act V, scene vii*